DINGHY & DAYBOAT

DIRECTORY

A comprehensive guide to sailing dinghies, keelboats and multihulls

Compiled

by

Diana van der Klugt

OPUS
BOOK PUBLISHING

Cover Design: Dave Steele
Cover Photographs:
Front cover - top: 17' Lune Whammel Boat
centre: Boss
bottom: Warp
Back cover - Laser fleet

Published by
OPUS Book Publishing Limited
Millhouse, Riseden Road, Wadhurst, East Sussex TN5 6NY.

First edition 1997

Copyright: Diana van der Klugt and Opus Book Publishing Ltd

ISBN 1 898574 04 9

Printed in Hong Kong through World Print Limited.

CONTENTS

INTRODUCTION

This book is designed as both an aid to identification - using the 'at a glance' index of sail insignia on pages 11 to 17 and as an 'in depth' guide to the vast range of sailing dinghies, dayboats, keelboats and multihulls which are all part of today's sailing scene.

For this book, we have included only open boats with no cabins designed for day sailing, although some of the keelboats have small cuddies and a number of dayboats are used for camping with the addition of a boom tent. The 180 entries in this book cover a huge range of sailing boats from small una-rigged singlehanders, to one-design classic keelboats, traditional dayboats, Olympic classes and racing catamarans.

There are over 150 detailed entries with colour illustrations showing the most popular classes or types: a further 39 brief entries cover the older, local and less well-known boats.

The meaning of terms used in the text is as follows:-

PN: Portsmouth Number (see p.7 for explanation)
LOA: overall length of boat
Beam: width of boat at widest point
Draught: depth of water required with/without centreplate/keel etc.
Mast height: height of mast above deck
Sail area: area of rig (mainsail, jib, mizzen etc)
Spinnaker: area of spinnaker
Weight: weight of boat either hull only or all up as specified
Construction: materials used in building
Designer: original designer of boat and date if known
Builder: main builder of boat (see p.183-188 for addresses)
Rig: type of rig (see p.8 for diagram)
No. of crew: number of crew for racing and/or carrying capacity of boat
No. built / registered: indication of the number of boats in this class
Class secretary: contact for further information on class

All measurements are given in both imperial and metric form.

GLOSSARY

Asymmetric spinnaker:
                  asymmetrically shaped downwind sail

Beam: width of boat at widest point

Bermudan: three cornered sail with luff held to mast

Bowsprit: spar extending out from bow of boat

Carvel: flush wooden planking

Centreboard: board, which swings up into a case, which can be raised and lowered to combat leeway

Cat rig: single sail (also called una rig)

Clinker: overlapping wooden planking (also called clench)

Cold-moulded: method of construction using strips of laminated wood bonded with cold glue

Daggerboard: board, which can be raised and lowered inside a case to combat leeway

Development class:
                  design of boat is fixed only within broad limits and is open to development

Double-chine: method of angled construction used in plywood building resulting in two angles running along either side of the boat

Draught: depth of water required with/without centreplate/keel etc.

Gaff: rig with spar aft of the mast at top of sail

Genoa: very large foresail which overlaps the mainsail

GRP: glass reinforced plastic

Gunter: rig with upright spar at top of mast

Hard-chine: method of angled construction used in plywood building resulting in an angle between the sides and the floor

High-aspect ratio:tall and narrow sail

Hot-moulded: method of construction using strips of laminated wood bonded with hot glue

Jib: foresail

Ketch: boat with two masts, the aft mast is inboard of the rudder head

Leeway: sideways movement of boat through water

LOA: overall length of boat

Low-aspect ratio:short and wide sail

Masthead rig: rig in which foresail reaches top of mast

Monohull: craft with only one hull

Multihull: craft with more than one hull

One-design: all boats are identical and built under strict class rules to ensure all hulls are equally competitive

Portsmouth Number:
    handicap number given under Portsmouth Yardstick scheme to allow competition between different classes
    PY: Primary number - regularly contested number
    SY: Secondary number - published number not as regularly contested as PY
    RN: Recorded number - number published on strength of limited information

Plane:
    when forward part of hull lifts out of water, thus giving increased boat speed

Pram:
    dinghy with bow board instead of stem

Restricted class:
    design of boat is fixed only within certain limits leaving other areas flexible

Scow-bow:
    rounded or sloping bow

Sloop:
    rig with one sail forward of the mast and the mainsail aft

Spinnaker:
    extra large parachute-shaped sail used forward of mast for downwind sailing

Spinnaker pole:
    pole which extends from bow of boat to hold the spinnaker

Stayed mast:
    mast supported by wire stays

Stern:
    back of boat

Swing keel:
    keel which can be swung up to reduce draught

Trapeze:
    wire attached to top of mast and used to support crew

Una rig:
    single sail (also called a cat-rig)

Unstayed mast:
    unsupported mast

Wings:
    crew supports attached to side of boat

Yawl:
    boat with two masts, the small after mast set aft of rudder head

Photograph Credits

The following photographs are copyright as follows:-

Barrow Boat	R. Barnard	Dart 18, Europe, Fireball
Beta, Contender, Nacra	Champion	Fourteen, Javelin
B 14E, 470, Raider	Strawberry Marketing	Tornado, Wayfarer Warwick Baker
Cadet	Chris Baker	National 12, Optimist
Cherub	Claire Spens Photography	Wineglass, Shearwater Eddie Mays
Devon Yawl	Peter Chesworth	Toy Alan Pear
18' Skiff, Signet	Ocean Images	*Dart* *Dart* are trademarks of
National 18	Carolyne Vines	Performance Sailcraft
Sunbeam	Hamo Thorneycroft	*Laser* *Laser* Europe Ltd.

Other photographs are reproduced by kind permission of Boatbuilders and Class Associations

RIGS

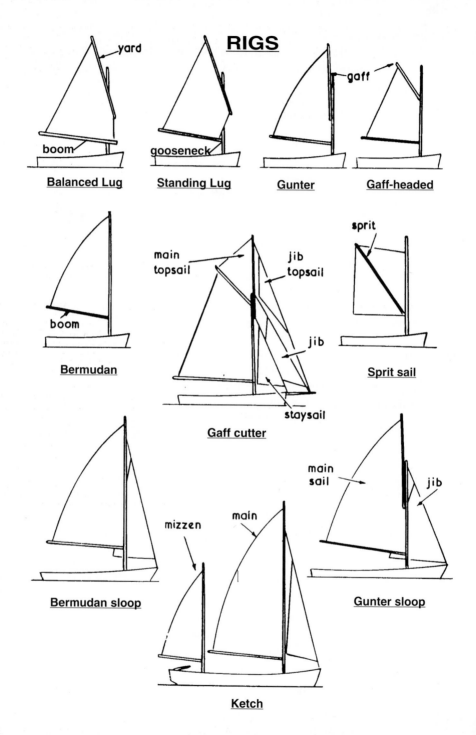

Balanced Lug — yard, boom

Standing Lug — gooseneck

Gunter — gaff

Gaff-headed

Bermudan — boom

Gaff cutter — main topsail, jib topsail, jib, staysail

Sprit sail — sprit

Bermudan sloop

Ketch — mizzen, main

Gunter sloop — main sail, jib

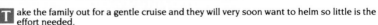

INSIGNIA 'AT-A-GLANCE'

13

ALBACORE

PN:1068 (PY)

LOA:	15'	4.57m
Beam:	5'	1.52m
Draught:	3'3"	1.0m (plate down)
Mast height:	19'	5.80m
Sail area:	125sq.ft.	11.65sq.m.
Spinnaker:	none	
Weight:	240lb	109kg hull
Construction:	wood/grp/composite	
Designer:	Uffa Fox	
Builder:	Chipstow Boatyard	
Rig:	bermudan sloop	
No. of crew:	two minimum	

No. built / registered: 7,900

Class secretary: Mrs D. Snowdon, 36 Simonside Grove, Ingleby Barwick, Stockton on Tees, TS 17 OPE

This round-bottomed, fast planing dinghy was developed in 1954 as a modified form of two earlier Uffa Fox designs: the 15' **Swordfish** (see p.142) and the smaller 12' **Firefly** (see p.59). It was designed to be a modern, light and seaworthy dinghy suitable for both family sailing and racing and is still among Britain's top 20 most active fleets.The class is restricted, thus the hull and sail plan remain unchanged although there is freedom for adopting new materials for hull, rig and sail construction and for modifying internal layout and control systems.The original hot-moulded wooden hulls were built by Fairey Marine but modern hulls are grp. A new lower cost grp hull with improved interior deck and layout is now being developed to upgrade the class by R.D.S. Ram Boats.

The name **Albacore** commemorated the Fairey Bomber Aircraft of the same name. The class achieved National status in 1963 and is still keenly raced at over 30 clubs.

A V BREEZE 6.0

PN: n/a

LOA:	19'8"	6.0m
Beam:	6' 2" - 9'10"	
	1.90m - 2.11m	
Draught:	5'3"	1.60m
Mast height:	n/a	
Sail area:	258.3sq.ft.	
	24sq.m.	
Spinnaker:	322.8sq.ft.	
	30sq.m.	
Weight:	484lb	220kg hull
Construction:	grp sandwich	
Designer:	Ian Howlett	
Builder:	Topper International	
Rig:	bermudan sloop	
No. of crew:	two/three	

No. built / registered: 30 (new class)

Class secretary: n/a

New two-man keelboat with lead-ballasted swing keel, fully-battened Mylar main, asymmetric spinnaker with swinging pole and sit-on racks for helmsman and crew. The **A V Breeze** sails like a modern dinghy and is powerful and responsive but without the risk of capsizing, the secure sit-out racks enabling her to be sailed upright She is capable of dynamic upwind performance but without the physical demands of many other asymmetrics, the sheet loads being light and the controls simple.The ideal combined crew weight for racing is approx. 33stone/210kg. The lifting keel is raised and lowered by a winch, enabling her to be launched like a dinghy.

AVOCET 12

PN: n/a

LOA:	12'6"	3.81m
Beam:	5'6"	1.68m
Draught:	7"	0.15m
Mast height:	12'	3.66m
Sail area:	79sq.ft.	7.30sq.m.
Spinnaker:	none	
Weight:	286lb	130kg all up
Construction:	plywood/epoxy	
Designer:	Christopher J Conway	
Builder:	Christopher J Conway	
Rig:	gunter	
No. of crew:	family	

No. built / registered: n/a

Class secretary: C.J.Conway,

32 Reymead Close, West Mersea,

Essex CO5 8DH

The traditional lines of this dinghy are based on those of local workboats but the modern construction methods have the added advantage of being low maintenance.The **Avocet** is ideal for singlehanded or family sailing with a manageable gunter rig and spacious cockpit.

BARROW BOAT 7'6"

PN: n/a

LOA:	7'6"	2.29m
Beam:	3' 7"	1.10m
Draught:	1'6"	0.46m
Mast height:	6'	1.83m
Sail area:	38sq.ft.	3.53sq.m.
Spinnaker:	none	
Weight:	55lb	22.7kg
Construction:	clinker ply	
Designer:	Colin Scattergood	
Builder:	The Barrowboat Co.	
Rig:	standing lug	
No. of crew:	one/two	

No. built / registered: 100+

Class secretary: 42 Barrington Place, Shepton Mallet, Somerset BA4 5GH

A traditional clinker boat made from modern materials and one of a range of sailing and rowing tenders supplied ready built or as kits including the 6', 8' and 12' **Barrow Boats.** These versatile dinghies are strong, pretty and very light, row and sail well and can take a 2hp outboard. The standing lug rig can be rolled up and stowed inside the boat which is car toppable.

BETA

PN: n/a

LOA:	13'4"	4.06m
Beam:	5' 11"	1.80m
Draught:	3'3"	1.0m
Mast height:	n/a	
Sail area:	123sq.ft.	11.35sq.m.
Gennaker:	100sq.ft.	9.25sq.m.
Weight:	175lb	80kg hull
Construction:	grp sandwich	
Designer:	Simon Cory	
Builder:	Brian Cory	
	Boatbuilders Ltd	
Rig:	bermudan sloop	
No. of crew:	two	
No. built / registered: new class 1995		
Class secretary: n/a		

Launched in 1995 and built to a strict one-design which ensures close racing and a high resale value, this is a simple hiking sailboat with gennaker suitable for lighter weight crews which is capable of giving a fast and exhilarating performance but which remains easy to handle at all times.The rocking spinnaker pole allows the boat to be sailed at lower angles downwind and together with the pivoting centreboard, this makes the boat ideal for sailing in shallow or restricted waters.The self-draining cockpit is comfortable and efficient with a central thwart allowing the crew to sit inboard in light winds.

B 14 E

B I4E

PN: n/a

LOA:	14'	4.25m
Beam:	6' 6.75"	2.0m
Draught:	1'8"	0.50m
Mast height:	23'9"	7.30m
Sail area:	188.3sq.ft.	17.50sq.m.
Spinnaker:	215sq.ft.	20sq.m.
Weight:	141lb	64kg hull
Construction:	grp foam sandwich	
Designer:	Julian Bethwaite	
Builder:	Rondar Raceboats	
Rig:	bermudan sloop	
No. of crew:	two	

No. built / registered: 660

Class secretary:Paul Taylor,

32 Cardinal Close, Caversham,

Reading Berks RG4 8BZ

This one-design, lightweight two-man skiff with asymmetric spinnaker has a planing hull shape, outriggers and a trapeze and was designed to bring the fun back into high-performance sailing. The boat is easily sailed both upwind and downwind and the excellent power to weight ratio and sophisticated rig enable a wide range of body weights to remain competitive. Ashore, the **B 14E** is easily towed, with the detachable wings pushed in or put on the car roof.

BLAZE

PN: n/a

LOA:	13'10"	4.20m
Beam:	6'7"	2.0m (incl. racks)
	4'11"	1.50m (excl. racks)
Draught:	n/a	
Mast height:	23'	7.0m
Sail area:	97sq.ft.	9.0sq.m.
Spinnaker:	none	
Weight:	143lb	65kg hull
Construction:	grp sandwich	
Designer:	Ian Howlett	
Builder:	Topper International	
Rig:	una bermudan	
No. of crew:	one	

No. built / registered: over 40

Class secretary: n/a

Newly introduced singlehander with a stayed mast and fully-battened sail allowing precise control of this fast but easily handled and versatile dinghy.The cockpit is deep but still self-draining and a pivoting centre-board makes quick manoeuvring and launching much easier. The simple open adjustable racks facilitate weight equalisation, enabling helmsmen of 9.5-13stone/60-83kg to race on equal terms.

BLUE PETER

PN: n/a

LOA:	8'	2.45m
Beam:	4'2"	1.78m
Draught:	2'	0.60m
	(plate down)	
Mast height:	15'4"	4.69m
Sail area:	38.5sq.ft.	3.57sq.m.
Spinnaker:	none	
Weight:	85lb	38.6kg
Construction:	grp	
Designer:	Ian Proctor	
Builder:	Anglo Marine Services	
Rig:	una bermudan	
No. of crew	two	

No. built / registered: 1180

Class secretary: Mrs Elaine Wright
14 Dunthorpe Road, Chatsworth Park,
Clacton on Sea, Essex CO16 8YN

A new small all-purpose dinghy, ideal for children to learn to row or sail in, which can double as a tender for up to four: the transom is reinforced to take an outboard motor. Carefully designed for safety with large areas of sealed in buoyancy, there is a recessed foredeck and the daggerboard case doubles as a rowing seat. The **Blue Peter** is lively and exhilarating to sail and the mast rotates for rapid roller-reefing. Ashore, she is light and easy to handle and readily cartoppable.

BOSS

PN: n/a

LOA:	16'1"	4.90m
Beam:	5'7"/7"10"	1.7/2.37m
Draught:	3'2"	1.0m
	(plate down)	
Mast height:	26'3"	8m
Sail area:	192sq.ft.	17.85sq.m
Spinnaker:	355sq.ft.	33sq.m
Weight:	176lb	80kg hull
Construction:	grp/carbon/foam	
Designer:	Ian Howlett & Jon Turner	
Builder:	Topper International	
Rig:	bermudan sloop	
No. of crew:	two	

No. built / registered: 107(new class)

Class secretary:Mike Pickering,

5 Park View, Tarrandean Lane,

Perranwell Station, Truro, Cornwalll

TR3 7NN

Introduced in 1994, this fast twin-trapeze asymmetric is a development of the **International 14** without the restrictive rules.The **Boss** has a fully-battened main and has inherent boat speed due to the low all-up weight. It produces top peformance but is also easy to sail and control. With a simple but effective weight equalisation system using adjustable racks, this is a boat in which women and lightweights can compete on an equal footing.

BOSUN

PN: 1196 (RN)

LOA:	14'	4.27m
Beam:	5'6"	1.68m
Draught:	3'3"	0.99m
	(plate down)	
Mast height:	21'6.5"	6.57m
Sail area:	115sq.ft.	10.68sq.m.
Spinnaker:	110sq.ft.	10.22sq.m.
Weight:	350lb	158.7kg min
Construction:	grp	
Designer:	Ian Proctor	
Builder:	R.Moore & Sons and	
	others	
Rig:	bermudan sloop	
No. of crew:	two	

No. built / registered: 2,000+

Class secretary: Capt. T.J. Norman-Walker, RNSA, 17 Pembroke Road, Portsmouth PO1 2NT

Designed in 1961 as a training/recreation boat for use by the Royal Navy, the **Bosun** has excellent buoyancy and is very strongly constructed, making her a safe boat to sail in the open sea. Although heavier than most contemporary dinghies, she performs well and is ideal for family cruising and tuition. The transom is strengthened to take an outboard motor and she is simple to maintain.

BRITISH MOTH

PN: 1183 (RN)

LOA:	11'	3.36m
Beam:	4'2"	1.25m
Draught:	3'9"	1.11m
Mast height:	19'7"	6.0m
Sail area:	85sq.ft.	8.0sq.m.
Spinnaker:	none	
Weight:	100lb	45kg min
Construction:	wood/grp/composite	
Designer:	Sydney Cheverton	
Builder:	Bassett Boatcraft, JEP	
	Marine/Brian Skinner	
Rig:	una bermudan	
No. of crew:	one	

No. built / registered: 830

Class secretary: Godfrey Clark,
28 Bassett Gardens, North Weald,
Essex CM16 6DB

One-design singlehander with simple hard-chine hull and fully-stayed rig designed in 1932 for sailing on Hyde Park Lake which later became established on the Brent Reservoir, becoming the classic restricted-waters boat. Originally designed for home construction from plans, modern materials and equipment are now used to maintain a modern racing dinghy with an efficient high aspect rig and lightweight manoeuvrable hull design which is responsive to sudden windshifts.The deep cockpit and carefully shaped sidedecks and high boom facilitate quick tacking and the freedom to adjust the rig and internal layout makes the class competitive for crews of all sizes and weights. Ashore, the light weight and simple rig make handling easy and with the two-piece mast, the boat can be cartopped. A junior sail plan, the **Mini-Moth** (64 sq.ft./6sq.m.) is available for small crews and for teaching purposes.

BUZZ

PN: 1007 (RN)

LOA:	13'9'''	4.20m
Beam:	6' 4"	1.92m
Draught:	3'6"	1.07m
Mast height:	22'6"	6.85m
Sail area:	138.3sq.ft.	12.85sq.m.
Spinnaker:	187.2sq.ft.	17.40sq.m.
Weight:	198lb	90kg hull
Construction:	grp/ foam sandwich	
Designer:	Ian Howlett/John Caig	
Builder:	Topper International	
Rig:	bermudan sloop	
No. of crew:	two	

No. built / registered: 250

Class secretary: John Caig,

71 High St, West Molesey Surrey

KT8 2LY

A new (1994) high-performance monohull with fully-battened Mylar rig, asymmetric spinnaker and single trapeze. A safe, fast and robust dinghy which is quick and easy to rig but less physically demanding to sail than many high-performance dinghies and therefore ideal for lightweight crews. Now used as a performance dinghy trainer at many sailing schools, the **Buzz** provides all the excitement and thrills of high-performance sailing while remaining controllable.

BYTE

PN: 1159 (SY)

LOA:	12'	3.65m
Beam:	4'4"	1.30m
Draught:	n/a	
Mast height:	17'2"	5.25m
Sail area:	60.3sq.ft.	5.60sq.m.
Spinnaker:	none	
Weight:	99lb	45kg hull
Construction:	grp sandwich	
Designer:	Ian Bruce	
Builder:	Topper International	
Rig:	una bermudan	
No. of crew:	one	

No. built / registered: 1,420

Class secretary: Kevin Moore,
22 Shetland Way, Fleet, Hants
GU13 8UD

This easily handled one-design singlehander introduced from North America in 1990, has a una rig on an unstayed mast. The loose-footed main and relatively high boom give plenty of headroom and the central traveller on the main sheet gives good power control. The **Byte** is a light dinghy, suitable for crews of 7-13stone/45-83kg, which is capable of high-performance while remaining very manageable and easy to right when capsized. Now raced at nearly 100 clubs, the **Byte** has plenty of room in the cockpit to sail two-up and is cartoppable, the two-part mast stowing easily.

CADET (INTERNATIONAL)

PN: 1432 (RN)

LOA:	10'6.75"	3.22m
Beam:	4'2"	1.27m
Draught:	5'5"	1.65m
Mast height:	15'5"	4.70m
Sail area:	55.5sq.ft.	5.16sq.m.
Spinnaker:	45.7sq.ft.	4.25sq.m.
Weight:	119lb	54kg
Construction:	wood/grp	
Designer:	Jack Holt	
Builder:	Rondar in wood	
	various in grp	
Rig:	bermudan sloop	
No. of crew:	two	

No. built / registered: 8,900

Class secretary: Secretary

129b Nantwich Road, Crewe

Cheshire CW2 6DG

Designed in 1947 expressly as a one-design racing dinghy for young people from 8-17 years old, the **Cadet** continues to fulfil this purpose, being the RYA approved youth training boat: some of the best-known sailors of today learnt to race in Cadets. With a hard-chine pram hull, she was one of the first home-built plywood dinghies although hulls are now built in grp. The **Cadet** is sailed in squadrons within over 23 clubs and there is a full calendar of open events.

CHERUB

PN: 1050 (RN)

LOA:	12'	3.66m
Beam:	5'	1.52m
Draught:	unrestricted	
Mast height:	20'9"	6.32m
Sail area:	125sq.ft.	11.61sq.m.
Spinnaker:	140sq.ft.	13.01sq.m.
Weight:	110lb	49.90kg hull
Construction:	all types- usually foam sandwich	
Designer:	various	
Builder:	various- mostly home construction	
Rig:	bermudan sloop	
No. of crew:	two	

No. built / registered: 2,700

Class President: Simon Roberts,
8 Plott Lane, Stretton-on-Dunsmore,
Nr Rugby, Warks

A fast and light two-man planing dinghy, this is a development class which originated from New Zealand. The first **Cherub** was built in the UK in 1956 and by 1962 all craft were fitted with a trapeze and spinnaker. The first UK design was launched in 1963, to be followed by many others but by the early 1980s the class was felt to be stagnating and a package of rule change proposals was put to the International Assoc. The failure of these changes to be accepted resulted in the breakaway of the UK fleet to form the UK Cherub class which has continued to develop, adopting the asymmetric spinnaker in 1991. The **Cherub** has a fully-battened main and is very fast downwind in a good breeze: she is most suitable for lighter weight crews of 17-22stone/108-140kg, especially mixed crews and needs skill and speed to sail well.

COMET

PN: 1173 (PY)

LOA:	11'4"	3.34m
Beam:	4'6"	1.37m
Draught:	4"-2'6"	0.1-0.76m
Mast height:	19'10"	6.05m
Sail area:	70sq.ft.	6.50sq.m.
Spinnaker:	none	
Weight:	110lb	50kg
Construction:	grp	
Designer:	Andrew Simmons	
Builder:	Comet Dinghies	
Rig:	una bermudan	
No. of crew:	one/two	

No. built / registered: 700+

Class secretary: Mrs N Gould,

32 The Dell, Kingsclere,

Nr Newbury, Berks RG15 8NL

One-design una-rig singlehander offering performance and versatility. The lightweight hull and powerful rig make her fast in light winds, planing well but remaining easy to control. The deep cockpit easily accommodates two adults for cruising and the sail can be easily reefed. The **Comet Mino** has a smaller rig (54sq.ft./5sq.m.) and a shorter, lighter mast for lightweights and youngsters. The active and friendly class is well established with racing fleets in many areas and is often used for training. The lightweight hull and two-piece mast make the **Comet** ideal for cartopping.

COMET DUO

PN: n/a

LOA:	12'2"	3.70m
Beam:	5'	1.52m
Draught:	6"-3'3"	0.15-1.0m
Mast height:	19'5"	5.90m
Sail area:	97sq.ft.	9.01sq.m.
Spinnaker:	none	
Weight:	194lb	88kg
Construction:	grp	
Designer:	Andrew Simmons	
Builder:	Comet Dinghies	
Rig:	bermudan sloop	
No. of crew:	two/three	

No. built / registered: 130

Class secretary:Frank Smith,
8 Landon Road, Herne Bay,
Kent CT6 6HP

A new (1990) multi-purpose dinghy, this well-balanced boat has plenty of cockpit space and an ample sail area with slab reefing on the mainsail and a roller furling jib, making her ideal for both family cruising, two-handed racing or singlehanded sailing. There is a large forward hatch for stowage and the optional extra of an outboard pad for a 4hp outboard. The hull is solid yet light making her easy to handle ashore.

COMET TRIO

PN: n/a

LOA:	15'	4.60m
Beam:	6'	1.83m
Draught:	8"-3'9"	0.2-1.15m
Mast height:	23'	7.0m
Sail area:	135sq.ft.	12.53sq.m.
Spinnaker:	100sq.ft.	9.28sq.m.
Weight:	295lb	134kg
Construction:	grp	
Designer:	Phil Morrison	
Builder:	Comet Dinghies	
Rig:	bermudan sloop	
No. of crew:	two for racing, four/five for cruising	

No. built / registered: 50 (new 1995)

Class secretary: c/o Comet Dinghies

A new general purpose dinghy with a roomy cockpit which performs well with up to 4/5 crew making it ideal for family cruising, two-handed racing and tuition. A complex reefing system with slab reefing on the main and a roller furling jib provides effective control in stronger winds and an asymmetric spinnaker on a telescopic bowsprit is available as an optional extra.

CONCEPT 302

PN: n/a

LOA:	9'11"	3.02m
Beam:	3'11"	1.20m
Draught:	2'1"	0.85m
Mast height:	15'2"	4.65m
Sail area:	55sq.ft.	5.1sq.m.
(junior class)	45sq ft	4.2sq.m.
Spinnaker:	none	
Weight:	70.4lb	32kg
Construction:	grp with carbon fibre unidirectional stringers	
Designer:	Tor Bakke	
Builder:	Concept Int (UK) Ltd. hulls built by Porter Bros.	
Rig:	una bermudan	
No. of crew:	one	
No. built / registered:	210 (mostly in Scandinavia)	
Class secretary:	c/o Concept Int (UK)	

A multi-purpose performance one-design singlehander from Norway which is lightweight but strong and available with two different rigs. With the Junior Class rig, the boat is ideal for juniors with a weight of 8-11stone/50-70kg, thus filling the gap between the **Optimist** (see p.114) and the **Laser** (see p.89). With the larger rig and asymmetric gennaker, the **Concept** can be successfully raced by two experienced beginners or one adult of up to approx. 13.5stone/85kg. The class rules include two separate classes and the junior rig can be upgraded at any time. The boat is unsinkable with a self-draining cockpit and quick and easy to rig: the fully pivoting rudder blade and centreboard facilitate beach launching and the dinghy is easily handled ashore and is cartoppable.

CONTENDER (INT.)

PN: 995(PY)

LOA:	16'	4.87m
Beam:	4' 8"	1.50m
Draught:	4'4"	1.40m
Mast height:	21'2"	6.46m
Sail area:	112sq.ft.	10.80sq.m.
Spinnaker:	none	
Weight:	183lb	83kg hull
Construction:	grp/composite	
Designer:	Ben Lexcen/Bob Miller (1967)	
Builder:	Rondar Raceboats/ Ridge Boats	
Rig:	una bermudan	
No. of crew:	one	

No. built / registered: 630 (UK)

Class secretary: Bernard Shapley, 111 Willingdon Road, Wood Green, London N22 6SE

A challenging high-performance one-design singlehander with a trapeze, sailed successfully by both men and women with weights from 8.5-15stone/55-95kg. The round-bottomed hull and comparatively large sail area enables the **Contender** to plane easily and she is especially fast on a reach.The class is well established and growing and was selected in 1967 as a potential Olympic succesor to the Finn. It was awarded International status in 1968 and there are fleets in more than twelve countries worldwide. Class rules are regularly reviewed to prohibit the use of exotic materials and expensive equipment, which helps to keep costs down.

CORNISH COBLE

PN: n/a

LOA:	19'	5.79m
Beam:	6'	1.83m
Draught:	7"/3'6"	0.18/1.07m
Mast height:	16'6"	5.02m
Sail area:	131sq.ft.	12.17sq.m.
Spinnaker:	none	
Weight:	600lb	272kg
Construction:	grp	
Designer:	Roger Dongray	
Builder:	Cornish Crabbers	
Rig:	standing lug	
No. of crew:	four to six	

No. built / registered: 360

Class secretary: n/a

A shallow-draught dayboat with a roomy cockpit easily sailed by beginners. The robust hull has a centreplate and twin skegs aft for grounding safely upright. The standing lug main is loose-footed and there is a flying jib. The **Coble** performs well and is easily handled and the roomy cockpit has ample space for up to six crew. Ashore, the spars will stow inside the boat which is easily launched and trailed.

CORNISH CORMORANT

PN: n/a

LOA:	12'3"	3.73m
Beam:	5' 7"	1.70m
Draught:	7"/3'6"	0.18/1.07m
Mast height:	14'	4.26m
Sail area:	88sq.ft.	8.18sq.m.
Spinnaker:	none	
Weight:	350lb	158.76kg
Construction:	grp	
Designer:	Roger Dongray	
Builder:	Cornish Crabbers	
Rig:	una gaff	
No. of crew:	up to four	

No. built / registered: 195

Class secretary: n/a

The smallest in the Cornish Crabber range, this cat-rigged dinghy is great fun to sail for adults and children with room for up to four in the cockpit. The ruggedly moulded hull has an integral centreboard case and built in buoyancy, the long foredeck and sidedecks keeping the boat dry and providing ample covered stowage space. The single gaff sail on the unstayed mast handles easily and can be stowed inside the boat. An optional boom tent is available. Ashore, the **Cormorant** is easily towed and launched.

CORNISH CRABBER

PN: n/a

LOA:	20'	6.09m
Beam:	6' 9"	2.06m
Draught:	1'7"/4'	0.48/1.22m
Mast height:	16'	4.87m
Sail area:	178sq.ft.	16.54sq.m.
Spinnaker:	90sq.ft.	8.36sq.m.
	(optional)	
Weight:	1400lb	635kg
Construction:	grp	
Designer:	Roger Dongray	
Builder:	Cornish Crabbers	
Rig:	gaff	
No. of crew:	four	
No. built / registered: 44		
Class secretary: n/a		

The ultimate dayboat with classic lines and excellent performance, the **Crabber** has a robust hull and roomy cockpit: she is shoal-draught with a lifting centre keel and rudder plates enabling her to dry out well on a mooring. The high peaked gaff rig has full control of sheeting and sail shape and is easily reefed; an optional spinnaker is also available. Ashore, the **Crabber** is easily trailed.

CRUZ

PN: n/a

LOA:	14' 3"	4.35m
Beam:	5' 8"	1.80m
Draught:	3' 8"	1.14m
	(plate down)	
Mast height:	18'	5.50m
Sail area:	111sq.ft	10.30 sq.m
Spinnaker:	none	
Weight:	264lb	120kg hull
Construction:	grp sandwich	
Designer:	Ian Howlett	
Builder:	Topper International	
Rig:	cat-ketch	
No. of crew:	family	
No. built / registered: n/a		
Class secretary: c/o Topper International		

Introduced in 1994, this 14' family dayboat has a robust and stable hull and roomy cockpit with ample watertight storage. She performs well under her simple unstayed cat-ketch rig with a single sail on each of her two unstayed masts, being fast but dry and can be easily sailed by two, although there is plenty of room for 4 or 5. She is easily handled ashore when the two-section mast can be stowed inside the hull.

The **Cruz Classic** has the same robust hull and roomy cockpit as the Cruz but with a fully-battened sloop rig (118.3sq.ft./11sq.m.), and an optional asymmetric spinnaker (156sq.ft./14.5sq.m.) with over-deck pole, she is designed for racing with a crew of two.

DEVON YAWL

PN: n/a

LOA:	16'	4.87m (plus 2'/0.6m bowsprit)
Beam:	6' 3.5"	1.92m
Draught:	4'6"	1.37m platedown, 11"/0.28m plate up
Mast height:	24'7"	7.50m
Sail area:	167sq.ft.	15.50sq.m.
Spinnaker:	none	
Weight:	950lb	432kg min
Construction:	grp simulated clinker	
Designer:	n/a	
Builder:	Devon Yawl Ltd	
Rig:	yawl	
No. of crew:	two to five	

No. built / registered: 256 in UK

Class secretary: Mr D Gouldsworthy
12 Meadow View Road, Boughton
Monchelsea, Maidstone ME17 4LH

An attractive all-purpose and seaworthy dayboat with an easily handled yawl rig, cast iron centreplate and classic grp simulated clinker hull. First launched in 1968, the design is based on the traditional lines of local fishing craft and the **Salcombe Yawl** (see p.126).With her roomy cockpit, she is ideal both as a family cruising boat and yet fast and responsive enough to perform well as an an all-weather racer.

The **Devon Dayboat** is a version of the yawl with an ample cuddy for overnight accommodation.

DRAGON (INTERNATIONAL)

PN: 1021 (RN)

LOA:	29'2"	8.89m
Beam:	6' 5"	1.95m
Draught:	3'11"	1.20m
Mast height:	26'6"	9.0m
Sail area:	286sq.ft.	26.6sq.m.
Spinnaker:	377sq.ft.	35sq.m.
Weight:	3740lb	1700kg all up
Construction:	grp/cold moulded/ strip planked	
Designer:	Johan Anker	
Builder:	Petticrow, Borresen, St Georges	
Rig:	bermudan sloop	
No. of crew:	three	

No. built / registered: 618 in UK

Class secretary: Sarah Threlfall,
110c Highbury Hill, London N5 1AT

Three-man keelboat, designed in 1929 by a Norwegian, this is one of Britain's most popular one-design classes with Royal and Olympic connections and is sailed in 28 countries throughout the world. It was an Olympic class from 1948-72 and in Britain, Prince Philip raced 'Bluebottle' for many years. Mainly sailed in the Solent, on the East Coast and in Scotland, with fleet racing at 11 UK venues, the early boats were built of mahogany carvel by the famous yards of McGruers, Woodnutts and Camper & Nicholson; now most are grp although some cold-moulded hulls are still built. Metal spars were introduced in 1971 and grp hulls in 1972. This is a classic design with the latest technology allowing all ages and sexes to compete.

DRASCOMBE DABBER

PN: n/a

LOA:	15'6"	4.72m
Beam:	5'10"	1.78m
Draught:	8" - 3'	0.2 - 0.91m
Mast height:	n/a	
Sail area:	118sq.ft.	10.96sq.m.
Spinnaker:	none	
Weight:	550lb	250kg all up
Construction:	grp	
Designer:	John Watkinson	
Builder:	Honnor Marine	
Rig:	yawl with standing lug	
No. of crew:	up to five	

No. built / registered: 880+

Class secretary: Luke Churchouse, Stoodley, Holne, Newton Abbot, Devon

Smallest of the yawl-rigged Drascombes, the **Dabber** is rigged with a bowsprit and a bumpkin and has plenty of room for up to 5 crew. She can also be rowed or motored with a 2-4hp outboard. Both the bowsprit and the bumpkin can be removed for transport and stowage. Ashore, she can be easily towed.

All Drascombes have the distinctive Lapstrake construction and tan sails.

DRASCOMBE LONGBOAT

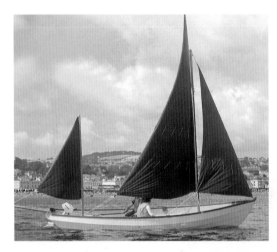

PN: n/a

LOA:	21'9"	6.63m
Beam:	6' 6"	2.0m
Draught:	1'-4'3"	0.3-1.27m
Mast height:	n/a	
Sail area:	172sq.ft.	15.97sq.m.
Spinnaker:	none	
Weight:	880lb	400kg
Construction:	grp	
Designer:	John Watkinson	
Builder:	Honnor Marine	
Rig:	gunter yawl	
No. of crew:	up to 10	

No. built / registered: 1010

Class secretary: Luke Churchouse, Stoodley, Holne, Newton Abbot, Devon

A larger gunter yawl in the Drascombe range, the **Longboat** is roomy and stable and ideal for fishing expeditions and coastal exploration. The shallow-draught kick-up rudder makes her ideal for exploring shallow water and a sprayhood and boat tent can be fitted for cruising.

The **Coaster** is based on the hull of the Longboat but with the addition of a small cabin and with a reduced rig of 164sq.ft/15.22sq.m. and can take up to six people.

The **Gig,** a yawl with a standing lug rig of 255sq.ft./23.72sq.m., is at 25'/7.62m LOA the largest boat in the Drascombe range and designed for use mainly as a training vessel taking a crew of up to twelve.

All have the typical Lapstrake construction and tan sails.

DRASCOMBE LUGGER

PN: n/a

LOA:	18'9"	5.72m
Beam:	6' 3"	1.90m
Draught:	10"/4'	0.25/1.22m
Mast height:	n/a	
Sail area:	132sq.ft.	12.26sq.m.
Spinnaker:	none	
Weight:	748lb	340kg all up
Construction:	grp	
Designer:	John Watkinson	
Builder:	Honnor Marine	
Rig:	gunter yawl	
No. of crew:	up to 7	

No. built / registered: 1,850

Class secretary: Luke Churchouse, Stoodley, Holne, Newton Abbot, Devon

The **Lugger** is a popular open dayboat typical of the Drascombe range; a trailer-sailer which is easy to launch and sail solo or with a crew. The loose-footed sails and sliding gunter rig make her easy to handle and ideal for inshore cruising and fishing trips when she can easily be run ashore for a landing. Optional extras include a sprayhood and boat tent for camping. She can also be rowed or motored with a 4-6hp outboard.

DRASCOMBE SCAFFIE

PN: n/a
LOA: 14'9" 4.5m
Beam: 5'9" 1.75m
Draught: 1'3" 0.37m
Mast height: n/a
Sail area: 100sq.ft. 9.30sq.m.
Spinnaker: none
Weight: 460lb 210kg all up
Construction: grp
Designer: John Watkinson
Builder: Honnor Marine
Rig: standing lug
No. of crew: up to four
No. built / registered: 420
Class secretary: Luke Churchouse,
Stoodley, Holne, Newton Abbot,
Devon

The **Scaffie** is a versatile boat with traditional lines which is suitable for rowing, motoring or sailing and the smallest in the Drascombe range. The cockpit is roomy, especially as there is no centreplate and the single standing lug sail is loose-footed making it safe and simple to handle: an optional sloop rig is available.

Also in the Drascombe range the **Skiff** is a traditional design which has been made in wood for 13 years and which is now available in grp. The rig is a sloop standing lug on an unstayed sitka spruce mast and there is room for a crew of two: other measurements are as follows:
LOA 14'9"/4.5m; BEAM 4'6"/1.4m; DRAUGHT 8"-2'6"/0.2-0.8m ; SAIL AREA 67'.75sq.ft./6.3 sq.m.; ALL UP WEIGHT 286lb/130kg

All Drascombes have the distinctive Lapstrake construction and tan sails.

EIGHTEEN FOOT SKIFF

PN: n/a

LOA:	18'	5.49m
Beam:	various	
Draught:	variable	
Mast height:	variable	
Sail area:	free	
Spinnaker:	free	
Weight:	181.5lb	82.5kg hull
Construction:	carbon epoxy on foam core	
Designer:	Julian Bethwaite (UK)	
Builder:	Ovington Boats	
Rig:	bermudan	
No. of crew:	three	

No. built / registered: 14 (UK)

Class secretary: Rob Dulson,
Sailspeed Promotions,
Unit 5, 62-70 Fowler Road, Hainault,
Ilford, Essex IG6 3UT

Australian-style high-performance dinghy with wings, bowsprit and asymmetric spinnaker, held to be the world's fastest sailing dinghy. A development class raced mainly in Australia but with a growing UK circuit.

EMSWORTH LUGGER

PN: n/a

LOA:	9'3"	2.82m
Beam:	4'1"	1.30m
Draught:	n/a	
Mast height:	8'9"	2.67m
Sail area:	47sq.ft.	4.40sq.m.
Spinnaker:	none	
Weight:	125lb	57kg hull
Construction:	grp	
Designer:	traditional	
Builder:	Dorado Boats	
Rig:	lug rig	
No. of crew:	one/two	
No. built / registered: n/a		
Class secretary: n/a		

A general purpose grp simulated clinker dinghy suitable for sailing, rowing or motoring with a 2hp outboard. Based on a local design, the hull form is stable and beamy with room for up to four people when under power or two when sailing and performs well in choppy seas. The balanced lug rig is easily managed, the mast stowing easily inside the boat, which is cartoppable.

ENTERPRISE (INT.)

E

PN: 1116 (PY)

LOA:	13'3"	4.05m
Beam:	5'4"	1.60m
Draught:	3'	0.90m
	(plate down)	
Mast height:	20'4"	6.20m
Sail area:	113sq.ft.	10.50sq.m.
Spinnaker:	none	
Weight:	207lb	94kg hull
Construction:	wood/grp/composite	
Designer:	Jack Holt	
Builder:	various	
Rig:	bermudan sloop	
No. of crew:	two	

No. built / registered: over 22,688

Class secretary:Bob Southworth, Crows Nest, 10 Fry Close, Hamble, Southampton SO31 4PF

A strict one-design class first launched in 1956 as a home-build kit boat, this is now one of the largest classes in the world, having gained International status in 1971, and a racing thoroughbred. The hull has a double-chine form, modern hulls now being of grp and all **Enterprises** have distinctive sky-blue sails. The class is suitable for crews of all types, being stable and roomy and with a simple internal layout. She has a powerful rig but no spinnaker or trapeze and is especially good for close tactical racing but is also popular with sailing schools and for family cruising when a reduced rig may be used.

ESTUARY ONE-DESIGN

PN: n/a

LOA:	18'	5.50m
Beam:	6'	1.83m
Draught:	11"	0.27m
Mast height:	31'	9.46m
Sail area:	210sq.ft.	19.53sq.m.
Spinnaker:	none	
Weight:	850lb	386kg hull
	(with centreplate)	

Construction: grp (originally wood)

Designer: Morgan Giles

Builder: various

Rig: bermudan sloop

No. of crew: three

No. built / registered: 114

Class secretary: A.A.Weber,
40 Walker Drive, Leigh-on-Sea,
Essex SS9 3QR

This class was formed by the amalgamation of the Thames Estuary One-Design class and the Essex One-Design class which had the same rig and sail areas but slightly different bow sections. Designed as fast racing day-boats and originally built of wood, boats are now built in grp, although older wooden boats are still able to race competitively: these boats are raced in the Thames Estuary.

ETCHELLS (INT.)

PN: n/a

LOA:	30'6"	9.20m
Beam:	6' 11.5"	2.10m
Draught:	4'6"	1.40m
Mast height:	32'6"	9.90m
Sail area:	291sq.ft.	27.0sq.m.
Spinnaker:	400sq.ft.	37.0sq.m.
Weight:	345lb	156.8kg
Construction:	grp	
Designer:	Skip Etchells	
Builder:	Petticrows	
Rig:	bermudan sloop	
No. of crew:	three	

No. built / registered: n/a

Class secretary: Jan Ford,

109 Mill Hill Road, Cowes

Isle of Wight, PO31 7

An exciting, fast, three-man racing keelboat which planes in a good breeze and is said to be lighter and faster than either the **Daring** (see p.177) or the **Dragon** (see p.46). Originally designed in 1966 as a contender for the new three-man Olympic keelboat class although the **Soling** (see p.133) was picked. In 1968, the first twelve boats were built in America and originally named Etchells 22 because of their 22' waterline length. The class was granted International status in 1972 and the name was changed to International Etchells in 1990. The class has an excellent racing programme with fleets at Cowes, Lymington, Burnham and in Scotland: the fleet at Cowes week usually numbers 40-50 boats.

EUROPE (INT.)

PN: 1145 (SY)

LOA:	11'	3.35m
Beam:	4'7.5"	1.38m
Draught:	n/a	
Mast height:	16'6"	5.03m
Sail area:	75sq.ft.	7.0sq.m.
Spinnaker:	none	
Weight:	99lb	45kg
Construction:	all methods	
Designer:	Alois Roland	
Builder:	Winner, Finnessa & others	
Rig:	una bermudan	
No. of crew:	one	

No. built / registered: 335

Class secretary: Sue Moss, 4 Andrews Close, Tunbridge Wells, Kent TN2 3PA

Now the women's Olympic singlehander class, the **Europe** was originally designed as the 'EUROPA Moth' to comply with the 1960 International Moth Class rules, but broke away from that development class to become an independent one-design class and changed its name. The class gained International status in 1976 and was chosen for the women's singlehanded event in the 1992 Olympics. The class is sailed in 29 countries.

The **Europe** is recommended for light crews of 7-12stone (45-75kg) and the rig can be adjusted to suit the individual's requirements. Construction can be amateur or professional. Ashore the boat is light and easily transported.

FINN (INTERNATIONAL)

PN: 1075 (RN)

LOA:	14'9"	4.50m
Beam:	4' 11.5"	1.51m
Draught:	2'11"	0.89m
	(plate down)	
Mast height:	21'4"	6.50m
Sail area:	108sq.ft.	10.0sq.m.
Spinnaker:	none	
Weight:	278lb	126kg hull
Construction:	wood/grp/composite	
Designer:	Rickard Sarby	
Builder:	Victor Boats (Devoti Finn) & others	
Rig:	una bermudan	
No. of crew:	one	

No. built / registered: 544 in UK

Class secretary: Robert Deaves,
113 Mell Road, Tollesbury, Maldon
Essex CM9 8SR

Designed in 1949 as the singlehander for the 1952 Olympics the class has participated in the Olympics ever since, now as the men's singlehander. The **Finn** is sailed in over 50 countries worldwide with very strong fleets in Europe. The class is one-design with a una rig on an unstayed mast but there is some variation in deck layout and internal fittings.The **Finn** is a very challenging boat to sail with excellent windward and very fast downwind performance, and is best suited to heavier crews (over 11.5stone/75kg). The unstayed rotating mast which can be of metal or carbon allows full control of the sail shape.

FIREBALL (INT.)

PN: 991 (PY)

LOA:	16'2"	4.93m
Beam:	4' 6"	1.37m
Draught:	4'	1.22m
Mast height:	22'3"	6.79m
Sail area:	123sq.ft.	11.43sq.m.
Spinnaker:	140sq.ft.	13.01sq.m.
Weight:	174.68lb	79.4kg hull
Construction:	wood/grp	
Designer:	Peter Milne	
Builder:	various	
Rig:	bermudan sloop	
No. of crew:	two	

No. built / registered: 14,530

Class secretary: Jackie Barker, Afflington Look Out Barn, Kingston, Wareham, Dorset BH20 5LR

An International high-performance one-design class designed in 1962 which with its lightweight hull, fully-controllable rig and trapeze is suitable for both men and women crews, enabling women to compete on equal terms at all levels.The **Fireball** provides exhilarating sailing at club, National and International levels and in all weather conditions.There are fireball fleets at over 55 clubs in the UK with over 21 National Class Associations worldwide. Hulls are now produced in grp to revised rules, allowing simplified production methods and resulting in much cheaper boats.

FIREFLY (NATIONAL)

PN: 1170 (SY)

LOA:	12'	3.65m
Beam:	4'8"	1.42m
Draught:	3'6"	1.07m
Mast height:	21'	6.40m
Sail area:	90sq.ft.	8.36sq.m.
Spinnaker:	none	
Weight:	163lb	74kg
Construction:	moulded veneer/grp	
Designer:	Uffa Fox	
Builder:	Porter Bros.	
Rig:	bermudan sloop	
No. of crew:	two	

No. built / registered: 3,600

Class secretary: Christine Hughes,
Linmoor Cottage, Highwood,
Ringwood, Hants BH24 3LE

A long-established one-design class originally launched in 1946 when the characteristic round-bottomed wooden hull was made of hot-moulded ply by Fairey Marine, the **Firefly** has been updated as a class but remains a strict one-design.There is no trapeze or spinnaker and she is easy for beginners to learn on while remaining competitive and exciting for more experienced racers. Although modern grp sandwich hulls are now available, many of the old wooden boats remain very competitive. Many top sailors started their career sailing **Fireflys** and the class is particularly popular as a team racing boat.

505 (INTERNATIONAL)

PN: 906(SY)

LOA:	16'6"	5.05m
Beam:	6' 2"	1.88m
Draught:	3'9"	1.15m
	approx.	
Mast height:	22'6"	6.85m
Sail area:	185.50sq.ft.	
	17.24sq.m.	
Spinnaker:	250sq.ft.	23.25sq.m.
Weight:	280.3lb	127.4kg all up
Construction:	wood/grp/kevlar/	
	carbon fibre	
Designer:	John Westall (1954)	
Builder:	Rondar Raceboats	
Rig:	bermudan sloop	
No. of crew:	two	

No. built / registered: 8,600

Class secretary: T. & G.Scarisbrick,
6 Charles St, Hemel Hempstead,
Herts HP1 1JH

One-design high-performance two man dinghy with trapeze actively sailed at many places in the UK and worldwide.The **505** is a large and powerful dinghy but light for her size which sails well in all conditions but is tactically demanding, requiring an experienced crew for successful racing. There is active International class racing in 12 different countries.

FLEETWIND

PN: 1264 (RN)

LOA:	12'1.5"	3.70m
Beam:	5'0"	1.80m
Draught:	3'0"	0.91m
	(centreboard down)	
Mast height:	20'	6.10m
Sail area:	95sq.ft.	8.83sq.m.
Spinnaker:	85sq.ft.	7.90sq.m.
Weight:	140lb	64kg hull
Construction:	ply/grp/composite	
Designer:	Alan Eckford	
Builder:	amateur	
Rig:	bermudan sloop	
No. of crew:	one/two	

No. built / registered: 690

Class secretary: Karen Little

Chertsey Road, Byfleet, Surrey

One-design class with hard-chine hull originally constructed of marine plywood but now mainly grp or composite The cockpit is long with variations in internal layout and low freeboard.The **Fleetwind** has a high-aspect ratio sail plan, the boom extending considerably further than the foot of the sail and planes well in moderate winds. She is easily handled ashore and is sailed mostly in the Midlands.

FLYER

PN: n/a

LOA:	14'0"	4.27m
Beam:	5' 5"	1.65m
Draught:	n/a	
Mast height:	n/a	
Sail area:	119sq.ft.	11.30sq.m.
Spinnaker:	158sq.ft.	15.00sq.m.
Weight:	220lb	100kg
Construction:	plywood	
Designer:	Roland Whitehead	
Builder:	Bell Woodworking	
Rig:	bermudan sloop	
No. of crew:	two	

No. built / registered: n/a

Class secretary: n/a

One-design boat designed for home-construction in plywood/epoxy from kit. The stable hull has a fine entry with powerful planing sections aft, high sides and broad gunwales. The high aspect ratio mainsail is fully-battened and the asymmetric spinnaker is set on a retractable bowsprit 4'7"/1.4m long. The **Flyer** is sailed with a trapeze and suits a combined crew weight of 127-191lb/20-30stone.

FLYING DUTCHMAN (INT.)

PN: 871 (RN)

LOA:	19'10.5"	6.05m
Beam:	5' 7"	1.68m
Draught:	3'7"	1.09m
Mast height:	23'	7.01m
Sail area:	200sq.ft.	18.58sq.m.
Spinnaker:	209sq.ft.	19.40sq.m.
Weight:	286lb	130kg
Construction:	moulded ply/grp	
Designer:	U van Essen	
Builder:	various	
Rig:	bermudan sloop	
No. of crew:	two	

No. built / registered: 379 (UK)

Class secretary: Peter Doran,
4 Westrup Close, Marston,
Oxford OX3 0HZ

Originating in Holland in 1951, and designed as a two-man racing dinghy suitable for International Championships, the **Flying Dutchman** soon attained International status becoming an Olympic class from 1960 until 1992. A high-performance racer with a trapeze and spinnaker, her light hull and large sail area make her a very fast boat with tremendous speed on all points of sailing requiring a fit and strong crew to sail well.

FLYING FIFTEEN (INT.)

PN: 1026 (PY)

LOA:	20'	6.09m
Beam:	5'	1.54m
Draught:	2'6"	0.76m
Mast height:	24'	7.10m
Sail area:	150sq.ft.	13.90sq.m.
Spinnaker:	150sq.ft.	13.90sq.m.
Weight:	306lb	136kg hull
	(ex. keel)	
Construction:	grp or wood	
Designer:	Uffa Fox (1947)	
Builder:	Ovington Boats,Coryn	
	One-Design & others	
Rig:	bermudan sloop	
No. of crew:	two	

No. built / registered: 3,568

Class secretary: Mrs Veronica Falat
Swans Cottage, Waveney Hill,
Oulton Broad, Lowestoft, Suffolk
NR32 3PR

One-design International keelboat class capable of outstanding performance, especially in strong winds, yet remaining responsive and easy to control and suitable for larger crews of 22-26stone/140-165kg. An ideal boat for day sailing, the **Flying Fifteen** is fast, comfortable and safe. Ashore, the boat is easy to rig and launch and can be easily trailed. One of the older classes, the original design has been modified by Chris Benedict and Ivan Coryn. The class is still expanding and there are fleets at over 40 clubs in the UK: there is also growing interest in the older boats for which Classic Events are organised.

49' ER

PN: n/a

LOA:	16'5"	4.99m
Beam:	9' 6"	2.90m
excl. racks	5'6"	1.69m
Draught:	4'11"	1.20m
Mast height:	26'6"	8.10m
Sail area:	228sq.ft.	21.20sq.m.
Spinnaker:	410sq.ft.	38sq.m.
Weight:	134lb	61kg hull
Construction:	epoxy/carbon	
Designer:	Julian Bethwaite	
Builder:	Dave Ovington (UK)	
Rig:	bermudan sloop	
No. of crew:	two	

No. built / registered: 30 (new class)

Class secretary: Peter Holton,

5 Barn Hatch Close, Lewes,

East Sussex

Launched in January 1996 in the UK, this 2-man skiff claims to be the fastest monohull in the world. In appearance, rather like a two-man version of the **18' Skiff** (see p.51), the **49'er** has a light hull with solid wings to encourage a feeling of security and which provide the basis for a weight equalisation system.The cockpit is quite bare with a minimum of controls, the main is fully-battened and the bowsprit short, the broad-shouldered shape of the asymmetric spinnaker being designed to lessen the sheet load. This is a strict one-design which requires a great deal of skill rather than physical strength to sail effectively. Ashore the solid wings slide in to allow the boat to be trailed at the legal maximum width.

405

PN: 1090 (RN)

LOA:	13'3.5"	4.05m
Beam:	4'6"	1.38m
Draught:	n/a	
Mast height:	n/a	
Sail area:	85sq.ft.	7.98sq.m.
Spinnaker:	95sq.ft.	8.80sq.m.
Weight:	149b	68kg hull
Construction:	grp sandwich	
Designer:	Chris Benedict	
Builder:	Hobie Cat	
Rig:	bermudan sloop	
No. of crew:	two	

No. built / registered: n/a

Class secretary: D Gibbon Esq.

Brook House, School Road,

Bagthorpe, Notts NG16 5HB

A new (1991) performance one-design dinghy designed for juniors of 12-16 years, who have already learnt to sail, to learn more sophisticated skills. The **405** has a forgiving hull shape which is easy to steer and an asymmetric spinnaker on a retractable pole and a trapeze, although a conventional spinnaker can also be used. The **405** is easy to sail but requires good teamwork to achieve high performance.The dinghy is now recognised by the RYA as its official intermediate training dinghy.

470 (INTERNATIONAL)

PN: 973 (SY)

LOA:	15'5"	4.70m
Beam:	5' 7"	1.68m
Draught:	3'5"	1.05m
Mast height:	22'4"	6.78m
Sail area:	137sq.ft.	12.70sq.m.
Spinnaker:	140sq.ft.	13.0sq.m.
Weight:	202.4lb	92kg hull
Construction:	grp	
Designer:	Andre Cornu	
Builder:	G.W.Parker	
Rig:	bermudan sloop	
No. of crew:	two	

No. built / registered: 780 (UK)

Class secretary: Katie Nurton,
Pound House, Cranborne, Dorset,
BH21 5PX

Launched at the 1964 Paris Boat Show and awarded International status in 1970, this high-performance International one-design dinghy is used as the Olympic doublehanded class for both men and women with an optimum helm weight of 8.5-11.2stone/54-65kg and crew weight of 9.5-11.5stone/60-73kg. The class is also popular for National and International training with over 30,000 boats worldwide and for club racing and recreational sailing. Under spinnaker and trapeze the **470** sails fast and planes easily and she is a good seaboat.

420 (INTERNATIONAL)

PN: 1086 (SY)
new rules

LOA:	13'9"	4.20m
Beam:	5' 7"	1.71m
Draught:	3'6"	1.06m
	(plate down)	
Mast height:	20'	6.10m
Sail area:	110sq.ft.	10.25sq.m.
Spinnaker:	97sq.ft.	9.02sq.m.
Weight:	176lb	80kg
Construction:	grp	
Designer:	Christian Maury	
Builder:	Rondar Raceboats	
Rig:	bermudan sloop	
No. of crew:	two	

No. built / registered: 48,500

Class secretary: Kent Dhonau,
5 Wellington Cottages, Colliers End,
Ware, Herts SG11 1EE

Strict one-design dinghy first introduced in France in 1960 and now an International class ideal for both beginners and experienced racers. The **420** is now recognised as the premier youth training dinghy and is exceptionally safe and easy to sail with a manageable rig yet capable of exciting performance with the trapeze and spinnaker. Ashore, the **420** is light and easily towed or put on the car roof. Rondar is building 420s to the new rules which allow modernisation of the deck layout.

FOURTEEN (INTERNATIONAL)

PN: 884(RN)

LOA:	14'	4.27m
Beam:	6'	1.83m
Draught:	unrestricted	
Mast height:	25'	7.63m
Sail area:	200sq.ft.	18.58sq.m.
Spinnaker:	unlimited	
Weight:	180lb	81.6kg
Construction:	any- usually	

sophisticated composite

Designer:	various
Builder:	Ovington Boats,
	Rowsell & Morrison,
	Jon Turner & others
Rig:	bermudan sloop
No. of crew:	two

No. built / registered: 1366

Class secretary: Karen Evans,
22 Queensbridge Park, Isleworth,
Middlesex TW7 7NB

A high-performance development class, dating from 1920s, it gained International status in 1928 and is the oldest International dinghy racing class and has been at the forefront of most new developments ever since. The first true planing dinghy, it is now sailed with two trapezes and a mast-head asymmetric spinnaker of unlimited size set on a retractable bowsprit. The use of composite or carbon fibre masts and the latest innovations in sail materials and cut means she is extremely fast and rule changes maintain her position as the top European development dinghy. New rules for Jan. 1996 allow a larger sail area, longer mast and a reduction in weight, leading to a lighter, slimmer and more powerful hull with a larger rig. There is a fully developed class racing structure with fleets in many countries. Classic 14s follow the 1986 rules and have a single trapeze and conventional spinnaker while Vintage 14s are even older! Because of the nature of the class, a modern 14 always represents the ultimate in dinghy development.

FOXER

PN: n/a		
LOA:	10'8"	3.25m
Beam:	4' 6"	1.37m
Draught:	n/a	
Mast height:	18'8"	5.60m
Sail area:	68sq.ft.	6.30sq.m.
Spinnaker:	none	
Weight:	160.6lb	73kg hull
Construction:	grp	
Designer:	David Thomas	
Builder:	Red Fox Yachts Ltd.	
Rig:	una/bermudan sloop	
No. of crew:	up to four	
No. built / registered: 56		
Class secretary: Mr C.Boot,		
37 Valley Walk, Croxley Green,		
Rickmansworth, Herts WD3 3TQ		

Versatile little dinghy which is fun to sail for all ages with a high freeboard, roomy cockpit, lots of buoyancy and a simple rig. With its distinctive red, white and black panelled sail, the **Foxer** has already been adopted by three principal South Coast yacht clubs and is seen to be a little faster than a **Topper** (see p.147) and significantly faster than a **Mirror** (see p.107). The hull is available with two rigs, the mono and the bermudan which are interchangeable. She can also be used as a tender under motor or oars. Ashore, the mast can be easily stowed in two sections and the hull is light and can be easily towed or put on the car.

GALAXY

PN: n/a

LOA:	16'	4.88m
Beam:	6' 4"	1.95m
Draught:	1'4"	0.40m with
	bilge keels	
Mast height:	n/a	
Sail area:	151sq.ft.	14.02sq.m.
Spinnaker:	183sq.ft.	17.0sq.m.
Weight:	302lb	137kg hull
Construction:	grp	
Designer:	Mark Giles	
Builder:	Giles Reinforced	
	Plastics Ltd.	
Rig:	bermudan sloop	
No. of crew:	two +	
No. built / registered: 2 (new class)		
Class secretary: none yet		

Designed to perform well as both a club racer and cruiser, the well-built roomy one-design hull has a centreboard and self-draining cockpit with several storage lockers. For the racer there is an asymmetric spinnaker with moveable pole to enhance downwind performance and flared topsides for sitting out in fresh conditions. As an optional extra, bilge keels of galvanised steel can be fitted into specially designed slots in the boat to enhance the stability of the cruising version and to enable the boat to dry out on a mooring.

GP14 (INTERNATIONAL)

PN: 1126 (PY)

LOA:	14'	4.27m
Beam:	5'	1.54m
Draught:	3'	0.91m
	(plate down)	
Mast height:	22'	6.80m
Sail area:	122sq.ft.	11.33sq.m.
Spinnaker:	90sq.ft.	8.40sq.m.
Weight:	293lb	133kg hull
Construction:	wood or grp/frp	
Designer:	Jack Holt	
Builder:	many	
Rig:	bermudan sloop	
No. of crew:	two	

No. built / registered: 13,450

Class secretary: Graham Knox, 129b Nantwich Road, Crewe, Cheshire CW2 6DG

A popular general purpose dinghy which was designed in 1950 as the *'Yachting World'* general purpose 14' dinghy: progressive but controlled development of the rules has allowed the class to incorporate up-to-date rigs and fittings whilst ensuring that old boats can still be competitive.There is a wide tolerance of all-up crew weight, from 20-25stone /127-159kg, a midi genoa allowing lighter crews to compete on a par with stronger crews. The class is raced at 300 clubs throughout the UK as well as worldwide and is also popular for teaching and family sailing. The Class Association has a membership of over 3,000 and is one of the largest in the country. Ashore, the light hull weight enables the boat to be handled and towed with ease.

GRADUATE (NATIONAL)

PN: 1170 (SY)

LOA:	12'6"	3.82m
Beam:	4'9"	1.43m
Draught:	3'8"	1.12m
	(plate down)	
Mast height:	18'	5.50m
Sail area:	90sq.ft.	8.36sq.m.
Spinnaker:	none	
Weight:	185lb	83.92kg
Construction:	wood/grp/composite	
Designer:	Wyche and Coppock	
Builder:	7'Oaks Boats	
Rig:	bermudan sloop	
No. of crew:	two	

No. built / registered: 2,980

Class secretary: S.Eaton,

43 Cherrytree Close, Southmoor,

Abingdon Oxon OX13 5BE

Originally designed in 1952 to provide cheap class racing, the **Graduate** is a strict one-design two-man class with flexibility in internal layout and fittings permitted. She is sailed at many clubs throughout the UK and suitable for cruising and racing. The **Graduate** is a popular choice for beginners and experienced sailors alike, being lively and exciting to sail, strong in light airs but controllable in a blow and is easily handled, performing well in mixed handicap races. The boat can be built from a kit or can be bought partly or ready finished. Ashore, she is easily handled and can be towed by most small cars.

GULL/ GULL SPIRIT

PN: 1361 (RN)

LOA:	11'	3.35m
Beam:	5'3"	1.60m
Draught:	3'	0.90m
	(plate down)	
Mast height:	18'8"	5.68m
Sail area:	70sq.ft.	6.50sq.m.
Spinnaker:	60sq.ft.	5.57sq.m.
Weight:	160lb	72.7kg
Construction:	grp/wood	
Designer:	Ian Proctor	
Builder:		Anglo Marine Services
Rig:		bermudan sloop
No. of crew:	two to four	

No. built / registered: 2,616

Class secretary: Gordon Williams, Crabbetts, Horning Road, Hoveton St John, Norwich NR12 8JW

Designed in 1956, the **Gull** was the first boat to receive the RYA's Approved Class status in 1963. There have been three different hull versions of this class, the original Mark 1 double-chine later being replaced by the Mark 111 round-bilged hull.A development of the original Gull class, the all grp **Gull Spirit** uses the classic Mark 1 double-chined hull but has a completely new interior incorporating built-in bouyancy, making it roomy and stable for all the family and a slightly larger sail area of 73 sq.ft./ 6.78 sq.m. There is an active racing fleet throughout the country. Ashore, the boat is easily handled and can be towed or put on the car roof.

HAWK 20

PN: n/a

LOA:	20'	6.10m
Beam:	7' 5"	2.26m
Draught:	4'3"	1.30m
	(plate down)	
Mast height:	27'8"	8.45m
Sail area:	220sq.ft.	20.44sq.m.
Spinnaker:	255sq.ft.	23.69sq.m.
Weight:	1800lb	816kg
Construction:	grp	
Designer:	Reid Marine	
Builder:	Reid Marine	
Rig:	bermudan sloop	
No. of crew:	up to six	

No. built / registered: 85

Class secretary:n/a

First launched in 1992, the **Hawk 20** is a high quality centreboard seago-ing dayboat which is self-draining, self-righting and unsinkable, due to her internal lead ballast and sealed buoyancy. With her powerful rig, she sails fast on all points of sailing,and planes readily. She can be easily sailed singlehanded and with her lifting keel is also ideal for exploring shallow water areas with the family and can be safely kept on a drying mooring. An outboard can be neatly accommodated in the engine well beneath the small after deck. Ashore, she is easy to trail and launch using the specially designed road trailer.

HERON

PN: 1363 (SY)

LOA:	11'3"	3.429m
Beam:	4' 6"	1.372m
Draught:	2'10"	0.864m
	(plate down)	
Mast height:	n/a	
Sail area:	69.8sq.ft.	6.50sq.m.
Spinnaker:	59sq.ft.	2.83sq.m.
Weight:	140lb	63.6kg
Construction:	wood/grp/composite	
Designer:	Jack Holt	
Builder:	Brian Cory	
	Boatbuilders Ltd	
Rig:	gunter/bermudan	
No. of crew:	two	

No. built / registered: 9,887

Class secretary:G.J.Perkins,
154 Red Lane, Paradise, Coventry
CV6 5EQ

Designed in 1951 for 'Yachting World', as a small and safe family boat big enough for two adults and two children, the **Heron** was originally intended for amateur construction and is of the same family as the **Cadet** (see p.34) and **GP14** (see p.72). A one-design class, the original rig was gunter so the spars could be stored inside the boat and the robust hull is hard-chine. Developments in the class now allow both metal and wooden spars, grp hulls and a bermudan rig: a larger rig (82 sq.ft./7.61 sq.m.) with genoa and spinnaker is available for racing. Many boats are still self-built and many of the early boats still continue to race competitively.The **Heron** is strong enough to take the ground on a drying mooring and is particularly popular as a training boat.

HEYLAND LUGGER

PN: n/a

LOA:	11'6"	3.50m
Beam:	4'9"	1.45m
Draught:	1'8"	0.51m
Mast height:	11'	3.40m
Sail area:	52sq.ft.	4.92sq.m.
Spinnaker:	none	
Weight:	170lb	77kg hull
Construction:	grp	
Designer:	Bill Bailiff	
Builder:	Heyland Marine	
Rig:	balanced lug	
No. of crew:	two/three	

No. built / registered: 119

Class secretary: n/a

This small **lugger** has a traditionally shaped grp simulated clinker hull and a simple balanced lug rig which together with the galvanised steel dagger-board gives good windward performance. She can also be rowed or motored and ashore is light and easy to transport on a trailer or car roof.

HEYLAND SWIFT

PN: n/a

LOA:	8'3"	2.50m
Beam:	4'5"	1.33m
Draught:	1'8"	0.51m
Mast height:	13'3"	4.14m
Sail area:	46sq.ft.	4.30sq.m.
Spinnaker:	none	
Weight:	85lb	39kg hull
Construction:	grp	
Designer:	Gerald Heyland	
Builder:	Heyland Marine	
Rig:	bermudan sloop	
No. of crew:	two/three	

No. built / registered: 215

Class secretary: n/a

The **Swift** is a bermudan rigged grp dinghy, a versatile craft with good stability and high freeboard. She can be rowed and motored and with her unstayed mast is easy to rig. Ashore she fits easily on the car roof, the jointed 2-piece mast is easily stowed.

HORNET (NATIONAL)

PN: 975 (SY)

LOA:	16'	4.89m
Beam:	4' 6"	1.4m
Draught:	3"-3'9"	0.75-1.0m
	(plate up/down)	
Mast height:	22'	6.7m
Sail area:	161sq.ft.	15.0sq.m.
Spinnaker:	132sq.ft.	12.3sq.m.
Weight:	277lb	126kg
Construction:	wood/grp/carbon fibre	
Designer:	Jack Holt	
Builder:	Malcolm Goodwin	
	Tim Coombe	
Rig:	bermudan sloop	
No. of crew:	two	

No. built / registered: 2,168

Class secretary: Cath Marchbanks, 34. Moatsole, Sandwich, Kent, CT13 9AU

Designed in 1952 under the sponsorship of 'Yachting World' as a high-performance one-design dinghy, the **Hornet** has a hard-chine and very narrow hull with a high-aspect rig and is sailed with a trapeze or sliding seat. The **Hornet** has a good weight-carrying capacity and with a choice of rig set-up, can be sailed by crews with a wide range of weight and strength. Crews of 17-25stone/108-160kg are competitive and mixed and female crews can compete with all male crews. If well looked after, boats can remain competitive for up to 20 years.

INTERNATIONAL 2.4 METRE

2.4

PN: n/a

LOA:	14'+	4.1+m
Beam:	2' 6"	0.80m
Draught:	3'3"	1.0m
Mast height:	18'	5.50m
Sail area:	70+sq.ft.	7+sq.m.
Spinnaker:	none	
Weight:	132lb	60kg hull
Construction:	wood/grp	
Designer:	various	
Builder:	Aldeburgh Boatyard	

Franklin-Eldridge Yachts & others

Rig:	bermudan sloop
No. of crew:	one

No. built / registered: 38 (UK)

Class secretary: R.F.Pierce,

High End House, Finsthwaite,

Ulverston, Cumbria LA12 8BN

The 2.4 metre is a singlehanded self-righting Mini 12m built to the same rating rule as the 12 metre and because of its heavy displacement, behaves like a large, well-canvassed yacht. The rig is a classic fractional rig with backstay and an optional self-tacking jib.The class is ideal for fleet or match racing with fleets at Windermere, Carsington and Queen Mary and appeals to a wide cross-section of sailors of all ages and levels of experience. Although not designed for disabled people, the class has been selected for the 2000 Paralympics.

INT. 10 SQ METRE CANOE

PN: 919 (RN)

LOA:	17'0"	5.18m
Beam:	3'5"	1.02m
Draught:	3'3"	1.0m
Mast height:	20'10"	6.36m
Sail area:	107.7sq.ft.10.0sq.m.	
Spinnaker:	none	
Weight:	138lb	63kg min
Construction:	no restriction	
Designer:	P.Nethercot (1973)	
Builder:	Razorback Boats &	
	amateur	
Rig:	bermudan sloop	
No. of crew:	one	

No. built / registered: 275 (UK)

Class secretary: Peter McLaren,

56 Bloomfield Avenue, Bath, Avon

BA2 3AE

Said to be the fastest singlehanded monohull sailing dinghy in the world the **International Canoe** has a strict one-design hull but sail plan and deck layout are open to restricted development. The hull is long and narrow with a distinctive canoe-shaped bow and stern and is relatively light and easily driven by her 10 sq.m. sail: the key to her performance is the sliding seat which enables the helmsman to put his weight 5'/1.5m out from the gunwhale and which also compensates for weight differences in the helm.The Canoe demands an agile crew and is challenging and exhilarating to sail and is sailed in more than ten countries around the world.

INTERNATIONAL MOTH

PN: 1022 (RN)

LOA (max):	11'	3.35m
Beam (max):	7'4"	2.25m
Draught:	unrestricted	
Mast height:	18'	6.25m
Sail area:	86.2sq.ft.	8.0sq.m.
Spinnaker:	none	
Weight:	unrestricted	
Construction:	various	
Designer:	various	
Builder:	various	
Rig:	una rig	
No. of crew:	one	

No. built / registered: 4,025

Class secretary: Ian Forsdike,

84 Heathcote Avenue, Hatfield, Herts

AL10 ORJ

A singlehanded development class with a lightweight narrow hull and wing outriggers, stayed mast and high-aspect rig with fully-battened sail. This is one of the oldest established but most progressive dinghy classes and the most popular International development class. Restrictions on length, beam, mast height and sail area have produced a wide variety of designs in all materials resulting in a steady improvement in performance. The class has given birth to others, such as the **British Moth** (see p.31) and the **Europe** (see p.56) which are both one-designs. The **International Moth** is a lively and challenging boat to sail, requiring a fit crew.

ISO

PN: 926 (RN)

LOA:	15'6"	4.74m
Beam:	5'8"/7'5"	1.75/2.25m
Draught:	n/a	
Mast height:	23'	7.0m
Sail area:	154sq.ft.	14.30sq.m.
Spinnaker:	202sq.ft.	18.80sq.m.
Weight:	220lb	100kg hull
Construction:	grp sandwich	
Designer:	John Caig & Ian Howlett (1992)	
Builder:	Topper International	
Rig:	bermudan sloop	
No. of crew:	two	

No. built / registered: 550

Class secretary: John Caig,
71 High Street, West Molesey,
Surrey KT8 2LY

A revolutionary one-design high-performance dinghy with wings, single trapeze and spinnaker, the **Iso** was the first inexpensive asymmetric spinnaker boat to be launched and the pioneer of weight eqalisation. The **Iso** is fast and sophisticated yet remains inexpensive because of its strict one-design rule. It has a wide appeal because it can be competitively raced by crews of from 20-26stone (127-165kg), the wings being easily detachable for heavier crews yet giving greater power to the lighter crew.The wide hull is stable and powerful and gives an exhilarating performance. There is a very active class association with National and International representation.

JAVELIN

PN: 926 (RN)

LOA:	17'7"	5.36m
Beam:	5' 6"	1.68m
Draught:	4'3"	1.30m
Mast height:	23'	7.01m
Sail area:	170sq.ft.	15.79sq.m.
Spinnaker:	170sq.ft.	15.79sq.m.
Weight:	260lb	118kg
Construction:	grp	
Designer:	Peter Milne	
Builder:	Northampton Sailboats	
Rig:	bermudan sloop	
No. of crew:	two	

No. built / registered: 560

Class secretary: Stephen Harris,
94, Aldwyn Crescent, Hazel Grove,
Stockport, Cheshire

This two-man racing class has a one-design hull and sail plan but no restrictions on fittings and is sailed with a trapeze and spinnaker. On the hull there is a distinctive knuckle moulded near the bow which makes the hull stiff and thows off spray making her a dry boat. The **Javelin** sails fast in light winds, tacks well and planes easily: she is also a good stable sea-boat.

JET

PN: n/a

LOA:	16'	4.90m
Beam:	6' 1"	1.86m
Draught:	4'3"	1.30m
Mast height:	23'9"	7.25m
Sail area:	200sq.ft.	18.60sq.m.
Spinnaker:	250sq.ft.	23.30sq.m.
Weight:	176lb	80kg
Construction:	grp foam sandwich	
Designer:	Phil Morrison	
Builder:	Nautivela	

(UK distributers Rowsell & Morrison)

Rig:	bermudan sloop
No. of crew:	two

No. built / registered: approx. 10
(new class)

Class secretary: c/o Nautivela,
Via Gardone 8, 20139 Milano, Italy

Italian strict one-design twin-trapeze skiff newly introduced to the UK. A light, fast but easy to handle boat with a generous sail area and asymmetric spinnaker and a sophisticated rig which can be finely tuned. She performs well in light winds due to her 'U' shaped hull section.

KESTREL

PN: 1041 (SY)

LOA:	15'7"	4.75m
Beam:	5' 6"	1.68m
Draught:	4'6"	1.37m
Mast height:	22'3"	6.78m
Sail area:	135sq.ft.	12.53sq.m.
Spinnaker:	120sq.ft.	11.14sq.m.
Weight:	265lb	120.2kg hull
Construction:	grp	
Designer:	Ian Proctor	
Builder:	Morton Boats	
Rig:	bermudan sloop	
No. of crew:	two	

No. built / registered: 1,526

Class secretary: David Hearsum,
8 Hall Lane, Wacton, Norfolk,
NR15 2UH

Originally designed in 1956, although the first **Kestrel** was not built until 1960. This one-design general purpose dinghy has a round-bottomed hull designed specifically to be built in grp and is sailed with a spinnaker. Because of the large sail area, the hull starts to plane in a moderate breeze. The optimum combined crew weight for racing is 24stone/89kg. A smaller cruising rig (135sq.ft./1.68sq.m.) is available.

KEYHAVEN SCOW

PN: n/a

LOA:	11'4"	3.47m
Beam:	4' 9"	1.46m
Draught:	2'6"	0.76m
	(plate down)	
Mast height:	11'	3.35m
Sail area:	70sq.ft.	6.50sq.m.
Spinnaker:	none	
Weight:	265lb	120.5kg
Construction:	grp	
Designer:	Wreyford Bros.	
Builder:	West Solent Boat	
	Builders	
Rig:	balanced lug	
No. of crew:	one/two	

No. built / registered: 228

Class secretary: West Solent Boat
Builders, Keyhaven, Milford-onSea,
Lymington, Hants SO41 OTR

The **Scow** is built to a traditional design, possibly originating in Holland. The modern **scow** has a distinctive cut-away forefoot, making her manoeuvrable and easy to tack, with firm bilges and a broad transom, Inherently stable, she is ideal for both family and competitive sailing as well as for rowing and for use as a tender. Ashore, she is easy to trail and launch. **Scow** classes exist along the Solent and Isle of Wight coast and are still raced regularly (see **Wight Scow** p.182).

LARK

PN: 1071 (PY)

LOA:	13'4"	4.06m
Beam:	5' 6"	1.68m
Draught:	3'9"	1.14m
Mast height:	22'	6.71m
Sail area:	105sq.ft.	9.75sq.m.
Spinnaker:	80sq.ft.	7.43sq.m.
Weight:	209lb	95kg
Construction:	grp sandwich	
Designer:	M.P.Jackson	
Builder:	G.W.Parker	
Rig:	bermudan sloop	
No. of crew:	two	

No. built / registered: 2,420

Class secretary: Steven Bolland,
37 Sidney Road, Hill Morton, Rugby,
CV22 5LB

One-design two-man racing dinghy with spinnaker first introduced in 1967. The **Lark** was designed to give good racing without making high demands on the crew's ability, the light hull and relatively small sail area giving a good speed. The boat is popular for novices and training and ideal for team racing: she is widely used by Universities and other organisations for match racing.

LASER (INTERNATIONAL)

PN: 1077 (PY)

LOA:	13'10.5"	4.23m
Beam:	4' 6"	1.37m
Draught:	3'2"	1.0m
Mast height:	21'2.25"	6.46m
Sail area:	76sq.ft.	7.06sq.m.
Spinnaker:	none	
Weight:	130lb	59kg
Construction:	grp	
Designer:	Bruce Kirby	
Builder:	Laser Centre	
Rig:	una bermudan	
No. of crew:	one	

No. built / registered: 155,000
worldwide

Class secretary: Brian Goulder,
18 Bath Road, Cowes, Isle of Wight,
PO31 4QN

First introduced in 1971, this strict one-design single-hander has been one of the most successful classes in the history of dinghy sailing. The **Laser,** which has now been selected as an Olympic class, is sailed in over 100 countries worldwide and there is an extensive racing programme of events with categories for women/youth and master sailors. The optimum helm weight is 11-14stone/70-90kg. With its loose-footed sail sleeved onto an unstayed mast, the **Laser** is simple to rig and virtually maintenance free: ashore it is light and easy to trail or put on the car roof.

The **Laser Radial** (RN 1099) is an International class and has the same hull as the Laser but has a reduced sail area of 62sq.ft./5.76sq.m. which is ideal for youth and women sailors (9.5-11stone/60-70kg). The rig is inter-changeable with that of the standard **Laser** and the **Laser 4.7m.** The **Laser 4.7m** (RN 1178)also shares the same hull but has a shorter mast and reduced sail area of 50.6sq.ft./4.7sq.m. and is more manageable for less experienced or lightweight sailors of 7-9stone/ 44-57kg.

LASER 2 (REGATTA)

PN:1031(PY)

LOA:	14'5"	4.39m
Beam:	4' 8"	1.42m
Draught:	3'4"	1.0m
Mast height:	16'5"	5.0m
Sail area:	124sq.ft.	11.52sq.m.
Spinnaker:	110sq.ft.	10.20sq.m.
Weight:	165lb	75kg
Construction:	grp	
Designer:	Frank Bethwaite (1980)	
Builder:	Laser Centre	
Rig:	bermudan sloop	
No. of crew:	two	

No. built / registered: 10,030

Class secretary: Terry Palmer,
31 Lowlands Road, Blackwater,
Camberley, Surrey GU17 OAL

A strict one-design two-man racing dinghy sailed with a trapeze and spin-naker. The **Laser 2** is the official IYRU 2 person youth boat. It is simple to rig and virtually maintenance free and car-toppable.

The **Laser Fun** has the same 4.39m hull as the **Laser 2** but is sailed with a gennaker (135sq.ft./12.4sq.m.) and has the option of a furling jib.

LASER 4000

PN: 906 (RN)

LOA:	15'3"	4.64m
Beam:	4'11"-7'6"	1.5-2.3m
Draught:	3'7"	1.10m
	(plate down)	
Mast height:	23'3"	7.10m
Sail area:	158.3sq.ft.	
	14.7sq.m.	
Gennaker:	184sq.ft.	17.1sq.m.
Weight:	176lb	80kg hull
Construction:	grp foam sandwich	
Designer:	Phil Morrison & Derek Clark	
Builder:	Laser Centre	
Rig:	bermudan sloop	
No. of crew:	two	

No. built / registered: 260

Class secretary: Mr T. Hartley,
5, Jackson Meadows, Barkisland
Halifax, W. Yorks, HX4 0UD

A new (1994) one-design two-person single trapeze and gennaker dinghy, exhilarating and comfortable to sail but easy to control with adjustable side racks providing a weight equalisation system enabling crews of different heights and weights to compete on equal terms. The deck layout is simple and efficient and the mainsail is fully-battened. This is a fast planing dinghy but with reduced sheet loads, giving the boat a wider appeal. The **Laser 4000** is Laser's rival to the **Iso** (see p.83).

LASER 5000

PN: 848 (RN)

LOA:	16'5"	5.0m
Beam:	6'2"-10'	1.9-3.05m
Draught:	4'	1.20m
Mast height:	27'9"	8.50m
Sail area:	227sq.ft.	21.1sq.m.
Spinnaker:	323sq.ft.	30sq.m.
Weight:	257lb	117kg hull
Construction:	grp	
Designer:	Phil Morrison	
Builder:	Laser Centre	
Rig:	bermudan sloop	
No. of crew:	two	

No. built / registered: 230

Class secretary: Christopher Burrough,
Banks Cottage, Devil's Highway,
Riseley, Berks RG7 1XS

New (1992) one-design two-man dinghy with twin-trapeze and asymmetric spinnaker, this is a high-performance boat with a planing hull and high-aspect ratio sail plan conceived for sailors with Olympic aspirations. The unique crew weight equalisation system ensures that boat speed is equal in all conditions for all crew weights of 22-28stone/140-180kg.

LASER 13

PN: n/a

LOA:	13'4"	4.05m
Beam:	5'8"	1.72m
Draught:	n/a	
Mast height:	n/a	
Sail area:	102sq.ft.	9.5sq.m.
Spinnaker:	113sq.ft.	10.5sq.m.
Weight:	300lb	136kg hull
Construction:	grp	
Designer:	Bruce Kirby	
Builder:	Laser Centre	
Rig:	bermudan sloop	
No. of crew:	two	

No. built / registered: 650

Class secretary: Mrs H. Lewis,
33, Acacia Drive, Sutton, Surrey,
SM3 9NJ

Introduced in 1989, the **Laser 13** is a smaller sister to the **Laser 16,** and is a quality family dinghy suitable for sailing, rowing or motoring. The roomy self-draining cockpit has room for up to 4 crew and there is a watertight storage locker.The generous main is easy to reef and the jib can be furled and an optional spinnaker is available. There is mainsail head buoyancy to prevent total inversion. The **Laser 13** is safe and stable, yet responsive to sail. Ashore, the mast splits into two for easy trailing with the purpose-built trailer.

LASER 16

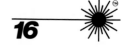

PN: n/a

LOA:	17'	5.19m
Beam:	6'9"	2.06m
Draught:	0'6"	0.18m
Mast height:	n/a	
Sail area:	151sq.ft.	14.02sq.m.
Spinnaker:	124sq.ft.	11.54sq.m.
Weight:	395lb	179.5kg
Construction:	grp	
Designer:	Bruce Kirby	
Builder:	Laser Centre	
Rig:	bermudan sloop	
No. of crew:	two/four	

No. built / registered: 1,000

Class secretary: Mrs H. Lewis,
33, Acacia Drive, Sutton, Surrey,
SM3 9NJ

Designed in 1988, this is a robustly constructed one-design quality day-boat ideal for family cruising with a very stable hull, large uncluttered cockpit, mainsail reefing, furling jib and forward watertight stowage area. The centreboard is fully retracting and the rudder lifts for easy beaching or exploration of shallow waters. A self-draining cockpit means she can be left on a mooring. Ashore, the **Laser 16** is easily launched and recovered using the custom-built trailer. A cockpit canopy and camping tent are available for overnight accommodation.

The **Laser 16 Unifurl** has the same hull with a unique furling mainsail.

LASER PICO

PN: n/a

LOA:	11'6"	3.50m
Beam:	4'8"	1.43m
Draught:	3'0"	0.92m
Mast height:	17'4"	5.30m
Sail area:	63.54sq.ft.5.9sq.m.	
Spinnaker:	none	
Weight:	121lb	55kg
Construction:	grp	
Designer:	Jo Richards	
Builder:	Laser Centre	
Rig:	una bermudan	
No. of crew:	one/two	
No. built / registered: n/a		
Class secretary:n/a		

A cartoppable fun dinghy with a robust hull, the **Laser Pico** is stable and easy to sail with a large self-draining cockpit. She is ideal for a child to sail alone or a jib (11.74sq.ft./1.09sq.m.) can be added for sailing two-up. She is simple and easy to rig. The sail is sleeved on an unstayed rotating mast and has a high boom and there are curved side decks and a simple kick-up rudder. The sail can be easily reefed by rolling it around the mast.

LEADER

PN: 1117 (RN)

LOA:	14'	4.27m
Beam:	5' 6"	1.69m
Draught:	3'6"	1.07m
Mast height:	22'	6.70m
Sail area:	118sq.ft.	10.96sq.m.
Spinnaker:	100sq.ft.	9.29sq.m.
Weight:	245lb	111.13kg
Construction:	grp/wood/composite	
Designer:	Gordon Pollard	
Builder:	Porter Bros. Fareham	
Rig:	bermudan sloop	
No. of crew:	two	

No. built / registered: 1,240

Class secretary: George Saffray,
7 Park View, Berkhampstead, Herts
HP4 3EY

Designed in 1962, this is a well-established one-design class. The **Leader** is a multi-purpose centreboard family dayboat which is also succesfully raced two-up, usually against the **Wayfarer** (see p.151) and **GP14** (see p.72). The boat is stable yet exciting to sail and easily handled and rigged with a tabernacle stepped mast. The **Leader 11** is a modified grp version of the Leader taken from new moulds with a revised interior layout.

LIGHTNING 368

PN: 1146 (SY)

LOA:	12'	3.68m
Beam:	4' 7"	1.38m
Draught:	n/a	
Mast height:	18'5"	5.6m
Sail area:	76sq.ft.	7.06sq.m.
Spinnaker:	none	
Weight:	120lb	54.5kg
Construction:	grp	
Designer:	Mark Giles	
Builder:	Giles Reinforced Plastics Ltd	
Rig:	una bermudan	
No. of crew:	one	

No. built / registered: 400

Class secretary: Sandy Broadbent, 6 Easby Close, Poynton, Cheshire, SK12 1YG

One-design singlehander introduced in 1977, which is quick and simple to rig, and lively but stable to sail. There is a flexible tapered mast and a una rig which can be finely controlled: upwind, she points high and tacks fast. The hull is strong but light with built-in buoyancy and a pivoting centreboard and there is a large self-draining cockpit giving room for two when cruising. The **Lightning** is considered good value for money for a singlehander working to a tight budget and is cartoppable.

LOCH BROOM POST BOAT

PN: n/a

LOA:	14'	4.27m
Beam:	6'0"	1.83m
Draught:	1'8"	0.51m
Mast height:	n/a	
Sail area:	117sq.ft.	10.87sq.m.
Spinnaker:	none	
Weight:	500lb	227kg
Construction:	grp with hardwood trim	
Designer:	traditional	
Builder:	Character Boats	
Rig:	standing lug with jib, or gaff cutter	
No. of crew:	one to five	

No. built / registered: n/a

Class secretary: n/a

A grp version of a traditional craft used over 100 years ago to deliver the mail from Ullapool around the shores of Loch Broom. Available with a choice of rigs, she has built-in buoyancy and a shallow keel. This beamy boat is stable and spacious with an uncluttered cockpit, ideal for family cruising on inland waters and is popular as a camping cruiser, the thwarts being removable. The boat has distinctive tan sails.

LONGSTONE 12

PN: n/a

LOA:	12'	3.66m
Beam:	4'10"	1.47m
Draught:	8"	0.20m
Mast height:	14'	4.27m
Sail area:	78sq.ft.	7.24sq.m.
Spinnaker:	none	
Weight:	400lb	181kg
Construction:	clinker wood	
Designer:	McNulty Boats	
Builder:	McNulty Boats	
Rig:	gaff	
No. of crew:	up to three	
No. built / registered: n/a		
Class secretary: c/o McNulty Boats		

One of the **Longstone** range of clinker built wooden sailing dinghies built by McNulty which range from a 7' (2.1m) LOA pram dinghy with a standing lug rig to the 16' (4.9m) LOA gaff-rigged **Longstone 16.**

LUNE LONGBOAT

PN: n/a

LOA:	17'8"	5.38m excl. bowsprit
Beam:	5'9"	1.75m
Draught:	2'0"	0.61m
Mast height:	18'6"	5.64m
Sail area:	160sq.ft.	14.87sq.m.
Spinnaker:	none	
Weight:	770lb	350kg incl. ballast
Construction:	grp with hardwood trim	
Designer:	traditional Scandinavian	
Builder:	Character Boats	
Rig:	various options including gaff cutter, ketch or yawl	
No. of crew:	up to eight	
No. built / registered: n/a		
Class secretary: n/a		

Traditional Scandinavian double-ended hull ideal for coastal cruising, the deep cockpit and ring deck making her an ideal, safe family boat. Her hull shape is easily driven and with her fixed keel she is stable and seaworthy. The cockpit is spacious and the various rig options mean she can be easily sailed singlehanded. Ashore she is easily towed by a medium sized car. The boat has distinctive tan sails.

LUNE PILOT 11'

PN: n/a

LOA:	11'0"	3.36m excl. bowsprit
Beam:	5'2"	1.58m
Draught:	1'3"	0.38m
Mast height:	11'0"	3.36m excl. yard
Sail area:	65sq.ft.	6.0sq.m.
Spinnaker:	none	
Weight:	290lb	132kg approx.
Construction:	grp with hardwood trim	
Designer:	traditional	
Builder:	Character Boats	
Rig:	standing lug with jib, or gaff cutter	
No. of crew:	one to three	
No. built / registered: n/a		
Class secretary: n/a		

A grp reproduction of a 1920s pilot punt used on the Lune estuary with a choice of rigs. This boat is deceptively roomy having no centreboard case but a shallow fixed keel with ballast, making her very stable and ideal for the small family or solo sailing. She is easy to launch and retrieve and can be towed behind a small car.

A slightly larger version of this boat is also available 12'6"/3.81m LOA carrying a sail area of 89sq ft/8.27sq m which can carry up to four people. Both boats have distinctive tan sails.

LUNE PILOT 14'6"

PN: n/a

LOA:	14'6"	4.41m excl. bowsprit
Beam:	5'4"	1.62m
Draught:	1'6"	0.46m
Mast height:	n/a	
Sail area:	120sq.ft.	11.25sq.m.
Spinnaker:	none	
Weight:	560lb	254kg incl. ballast
Construction:	grp with hardwood trim	
Designer:	traditional	
Builder:	Character Boats	
Rig:	standing lug with jib, or gaff cutter	
No. of crew:	up to five	
No. built / registered: n/a		
Class secretary: n/a		

A reproduction of a 1920s pilot boat designed to sail well to windward and to row easily in what were often difficult sea conditions. A seaworthy boat which performs well, she has a spacious uncluttered cockpit with a shallow fixed keel giving great stability and is ideal for family day sailing and even camping cruising under the optional boom tent. The boat has distinctive tan sails.

LUNE WHAMMEL BOAT

PN: n/a

LOA:	17'0"	5.14m excl. bowsprit
Beam:	6'0"	1.84m
Draught:	1'8"	0.50m
Mast height:	18'0"	5.49m excl. yard
Sail area:	160sq.ft.	14.87sq.m.
Spinnaker:	none	
Weight:	1000lb	454kg incl. ballast
Construction:	grp with hardwood trim	
Designer:	traditional	
Builder:	Character Boats	
Rig:	standing lug with jib, or gaff cutter	

No. of crew: up to ten

No. built / registered: n/a

Class secretary: n/a

Designed as a pleasure yacht at the turn of the century and based on the proven hull lines of the fast salmon fishing boats. With their large sail area they are renowned for their fast sailing performance even in the lightest of airs, which makes them popular with the experienced sailor. With a long shallow keel instead of a centreplate, the cockpit is left uncluttered affording a large space for groups or camping cruising. This boat can be left on a tidal mooring or can be towed by a larger car, using the purpose-designed trailer which facilitates easy launching and recovery. The boat has distinctive tan sails.

MARAUDER

PN: 1042 (RN)

LOA:	14'6"	4.42m
Beam:	5' 6"	1.68m
Draught:	3'7"	1.10m
Mast height:	19'8"	6.0m
Sail area:	150sq.ft.	13.90sq.m.
Spinnaker:	150sq.ft.	13.90sq.m.
Weight:	187lb	85kg hull
Construction:	wood/composite foam	
Designer:	Peter Milne	
Builder:	Ian Ridge	
Rig:	bermudan sloop	
No. of crew:	two	

No. built / registered: 1,008

Class secretary: John Marston, Cauldcotts Farmhouse, Anstruther, Fife, Scotland KY10 3JU

First introduced in 1970 and originally known as the **Mirror 14**, the **Marauder** is a two-man performance racing dinghy sailed with spinnaker and trapeze. The hull, which was originally designed for the stitch and glue method of construction in plywood has a hard-chine aft but is rounded forward and there are wedge-shaped bilge keels fitted aft which improve planing performance.

MERLIN ROCKET

PN: 1018 (SY)

LOA:	14'	4.27m
Beam:	7' 2"	2.20m
Draught:	n/a	
Mast height:	24'	7.0m max.
Sail area:	102sq.ft.	10.20sq.m.
Spinnaker:	70sq.ft.	7.0sq.m.
Weight:	217lb	98.43kg
Construction:	wood/foam sandwich	
Designer:	various	
Builder:	various	
Rig:	bermudan sloop	
No. of crew:	two	

No. built / registered: 3,543

Class secretary: Judith Massey,
12 Rowhills, Heath End, Farnham,
Surrey GU9 9AT

The Merlin-Rocket class was formed in 1951 by the amalgamation of two immediately post-war classes: the **Merlin**, designed by Jack Holt in 1945 for river sailing was based on the **National 12** (see p.109) while the **Rocket**, designed by Wyche & Coppock had a clinker hull similar to the **International 14** (see p.69) with a larger sail area and beam than the **Merlin** and was primarily designed for sea sailing. The class is a highly developed restricted class sailed with a spinnaker but no trapeze and is fast and fun to sail in all conditions being light and manageable. Because it is a development class, new ideas are constantly appearing thus, although the class is now over 50 years old, it is still at the forefront of high-performance dinghy sailing. There is a 'vintage wing' of the class association for older boats.

MIRACLE

PN: 1173 (SY)

LOA:	12'9.5"	3.90m
Beam:	5' 2.5"	1.59m
Draught:	3'6"	1.07m
	(plate down)	
Mast height:	19'2"	5.90m
Sail area:	95sq.ft.	8.90sq.m.
Spinnaker:	40sq.ft.	3.78sq.m.
Weight:	130lb	59kg hull
Construction:	wood/grp/composite	
Designer:	Jack Holt & Barry Read	
Builder:	Bell Woodworking	
Rig:	bermudan sloop	
No. of crew:	two	

No. built / registered: 3,780

Class secretary: Paul Butler,
36 Bitteswell Road, Lutterworth,
Leics LE17 4EY

A fast and versatile one-design dinghy introduced in 1975 suitable for family sailing or for racing two-up. With a wide beam, flat cross-section and double-chine hull, she is stable, spacious and easy to sail and her light hull is easily handled ashore. The **Miracle** is available in kit form for home completion or can be bought completed in wood, grp or composite. **Miracles** are sailed at over 60 clubs throughout the country and hold their price well.

MIRROR (INTERNATIONAL)

PN: 1382 (PY)

LOA:	10'10"	3.30m
Beam:	4' 7"	1.40m
Draught:	2' 6"	0.76m
	(board down)	
Mast height:	10'8"	3.30m
Gaff Length:	9'3"	2.80m
Sail area:	69sq.ft.	6.53sq.m.
Spinnaker:	47sq.ft.	4.4sq.m.
Weight:	98lb	45.50kg
Construction:	wood/grp/composite	
Designer:	Jack Holt & Barry Bucknell	
Builder:	Bell Woodworking	
Rig:	gunter	
No. of crew:	two	

No. built / registered: 70,000

Class secretary:John Golding, 311 Green Lane, New Eltham SE9 3TB

One of the most popular dinghies of all times, this small one-design pram dinghy was designed in 1962 for home construction by the 'stitch and glue' method and sponsored by the *'Daily Mirror'*. The **Mirror** is a stable family boat which can be rowed or motored with four or five aboard and which is actively raced both two-up and singlehanded (with a PN of 1362 (SY)). It is an RYA approved youth class, many top sailors having started in Mirrors and became an International Class in 1989.The **Mirror** is easily recognised by her distinctive red sails, hard-chine hull and pram bow. She is now available in kit form or partly or fully completed in ply and/or grp. Ashore, the hull is light and easily handled, the gunter rig enabling the spars to be stowed inside the boat for ease of transport.

NATIONAL EIGHTEEN

PN: 988 (RN)

LOA:	18'	5.49m
Beam:	6'	1.83m min.
Draught:	1'6"/5'	0.46/1.5m
	(plate up/plate down)	
Mast height:	28'	8.54m
Sail area:	240sq.ft.	22.30sq.m
Spinnaker:	190sq.ft.	17.65sq.m.
Weight:	550lb	250kg
(reducing to	500lb	227kg)
Construction:	wood or grp	
Designer:	Uffa Fox (1938) Ian	
	Proctor (1968)	
Builder:	various	
Rig:	bermudan sloop	
No. of crew:	two or three max.	

No. built / registered: 350

Class secretary: D.B.Newman,

4 Cedar Heights, Petersham

TN10 7AE

Commissioned in 1938 by 'Yachting World' this half-decked restricted class was designed as a safe, stable and seaworthy cruising boat yet a fast and exciting boat to race and is claimed to be faster than the **Dragon** (see p.46) and the **Swallow** (see p.141). A rule change in 1968 allowed the use of grp and other modern materials to an Ian Proctor design. The **Eighteen** is a specialised dinghy carrying a large sail area which is challenging to race yet which can also be cruised with up to six people aboard or sailed singlehanded in light weather: it has always been a fairly small class.

NATIONAL TWELVE

PN: 1098 (SY)

LOA:	12'	3.66m
Beam:	6' 6"	2.0m
Draught:	4'	1.22m
Mast height:	20'	6.10m
Sail area:	90sq.ft.	8.36sq.m.
Spinnaker:	none	
Weight:	176lb	80kg min.
Construction:	all types	
Designer:	various	
Builder:	various	
Rig:	bermudan sloop	
No. of crew:	two	

No. built / registered: 3,416

Class secretary: Mrs J Bloor,

52d Shaw Lane, Holbrook,

Derbyshire DE56 0TG

A highly developed two-man restricted class with minimal limitations which was introduced in 1936 as a small and cheap racing boat to act as a feeder for the **International 14** class (see p.69). Originally built of wooden clinker with a narrow beam she is now built using modern materials and has a wide beam. The **Twelve** is light, responsive and exhilarating to sail, requiring a skilled and agile crew to sail well: however, she is also manageable for the less experienced crew. The class is highly competitively raced around the country: older boats are not competitive with newer ones so there is a 'vintage section' for these boats.

NIMBUS

PN: n/a

LOA:	10'10"	3.30m
Beam:	4'	1.22m
Draught:	n/a	
Mast height:	n/a	
Sail area:	55sq.ft.	5.14sq.m.
Spinnaker:	none	
Weight:	85lb	38.5kg
Construction:	grp	
Designer:	Mark Giles	
Builder:	Giles Reinforced	
	Plastics Ltd.	
Rig:	una bermudan	
No. of crew:	one	

No. built / registered: 18

Class secretary: none as yet

A new (1985) general-purpose inexpensive singlehander dinghy with a sleek hull and self-draining cockpit suitable for both fun sailing and for racing. The fine bow slices through choppy water and the boat points high, planes easily and gybes smoothly. The **Nimbus** is simple and easy to rig, the main reefing around the mast if required, and is ideal for crews of 5-11+stone/32-72kg. Ashore, the boat is easy and light to transport, the jointed mast stowing easily inside the hull.

NORFOLK ONE DESIGN DINGHY

PN: n/a

LOA:	14'	4.27m
Beam:	5' 4.5"	1.65m
Draught:	7"-3'9"	0.18-1.16m
Mast height:	12'	3.66m
Sail area:	132sq.ft.	12.26sq.m.
Spinnaker:	none	
Weight:	n/a	
Construction:	wood	
Designer:	Herbert Woods	
Builder:	Herbert Woods,	
	Potter Heigham	
Rig:	sliding gunter	
No. of crew:	two	

No. built / registered: 86

Class secretary: Mrs M.Bushell,
184 Christchurch Road, Norwich,
Norfolk NR2 3PJ

One-design dinghy sponsored by the Broads Motor Boat and Sailing Club in 1931 and still keenly raced on the Broads. All the boats are clench built of mahogany on oak timbers and all have sails made by Jeckells. Terylene sails were permitted in the 1950s but spinnakers are not allowed, nor is it permitted to pole out the jib. Unusually, when racing, all boats have to reef if the reefing signal is hoisted. Of the 86 dinghies which have been built, 81 are still around.

NORFOLK PUNT

PN: 908 (RN)

LOA:	22'2"	6.76m max
Beam:	6'	1.83m max
Draught:	not measured	
Mast height:	not measured	
Sail area:	176sq.ft.	16.35sq.m.
Spinnaker:	unlimited	
Weight:	220lb	100kg min
	(hull only)	
Construction:	optional	
Designer:	various	
Builder:	various	
Rig:	bermudan sloop	
No. of crew:	optional	
No. built / registered: 91		

Class secretary: Richard Sadler,
9 Market Place, Hingham, Norfolk
NR9 4AF

This development class is concentrated on the Norfolk Broads and includes many boats built before World War 2 with an internal handicap system used to keep the older boats competitive.The class developed from gun punts used by wildfowlers on the Broads with Stewart Morris winning the first recorded punt race in 1923. Boats, many of which are still home built, originally had clinker sides and carvel bottoms and were gaff rigged but in 1952 Wyche and Coppock were commissioned to design a hard-chine hull for construction in plywood and from 1952-85 all punts were built to this design. A trapeze for the crew was permitted in 1957 and a second in 1984. In 1977 a grp version of the design was produced and in 1985 the class decided to revert to development class status with new rules for the hull: in 1988 the first design to these rules was produced by Phil Morrison. The rules have been updated to allow fully-battened Mylar rigs and the use of an asymmetric spinnaker set on a retractable bowsprit is undergoing a trial period.

OK (INTERNATIONAL)

PN: 1113 (SY)

LOA:	13'	4.0m
Beam:	4' 8"	1.42m
Draught:	1'8"	0.50m
Mast height:	20'	6.20m
Sail area:	90sq.ft.	8.50sq.m.
Spinnaker:	none	
Weight:	144lb	72kg hull
Construction:	wood/grp/composite	
Designer:	Knud Olsen	
Builder:	numerous	
Rig:	una bermudan	
No. of crew:	one	

No. built / registered: 2,081 in UK
15,000 worldwide

Class secretary: Mr A Atkin,
52 Goodliffe Gardens, Tilehurst,
Reading RG3 6FZ

Designed in 1957 as a light, responsive and fast one-design single-handed dinghy suitable for plywood construction, the name **OK** is the designer's initials reversed! Awarded International status in 1974, the class is very popular worldwide and is now built in grp as well as plywood although all types of construction are equally competitive. Choice of mast, sail and fittings is open, enabling crews to rig for their own physique thus making the class suitable for a wide range of crews of all weights and ages. Strict controls on the hull shape ensure the boat has a long competitive life. There is active club racing throughout the UK with a Junior Championship and a Veteran Championship. The lightweight hull is cartoppable.

OPTIMIST

PN: 1646 (SY)

LOA:	7'7"	2.3m
Beam:	3' 8.5"	1.13m
Draught:	2'7"	0.81m
Mast height:	7' 8.5"	2.35m
Sail area:	35sq.ft.	3.25sq.m.
Spinnaker:	none	
Weight:	77lb	34.93kg
Construction:	plywood/grp	
Designer:	Clark Miills	
Builder:	Moores of Wroxham	
	Bell Woodworking	
Rig:	spritsail	
No. of crew:	one	

No. built / registered: 4,400 in UK

Class secretary:A.C.Burdall,
Longacre, 2 Fernham Road,
Farringdon, Oxon SN7 7JY

Designed in Florida in 1947 as a cheap-to-build and fun-to-sail beginner's boat for the under 16s and granted International status in 1973, the **Optimist** is recognised worldwide as one of the best boats for introducing children to sailing with its easily handled simple spritsail rig. Over 60 clubs in the UK have **Optimist** flotillas and the class is recommended by the RYA for getting youngsters sailing. From March 1996 a new strict one-design grp **Optimist** is being introduced: all new grp boats will have to conform to these rules and will therefore be identical. Ashore, the **Optimist** is light and easily transported on the car roof.

OSPREY (NATIONAL)

PN: 938 (SY)

LOA:	17'6"	5.83m
Beam:	5' 9"	1.63m
Draught:	4'10"	1.47m
Mast height:	23'7"	7.20m
Sail area:	150sq.ft.	13.94sq.m.
Spinnaker:	185sq.ft.	17.19sq.m.
Weight:	294.58lb	133.9kg hull

Construction: wood/grp/composite

Designer: Ian Proctor

Builder: Porter Brothers, Chipstow Boatyards, Arnott Dobson, John Claridge

Rig: bermudan sloop

No. of crew: two/three

No. built / registered: 1,300

Class secretary: Nick Jones, 2 Tyne Close, Flitwick, Bedford MK45 1DG

High-performance one-design usually sailed two-up with trapeze and spinnaker. In 1953, Ian Proctor's prototype of this class won the Round the Island dinghy race against 190 starters from all classes. The **Osprey** has a treble-chine hull and is decked fore and aft and was originally designed for amateur assembly from prefabricated parts: she is fast and planes easily yet also has a reputation as a seaworthy boat. Changes to the class rules have allowed some modifications to be made to the Mark 11 boats.

OTTER

PN: 1270 (RN)

LOA:	11'11"	3.67m
Beam:	4' 10"	1.49m
Draught:	3'6"	1.07m
Mast height:	17'2.5"	5.30m
Sail area:	75sq.ft.	7.0sq.m.
Spinnaker:	70sq.ft.	6.53sq.m.
Weight:	165lb	74kg hull
Construction:	grp	
Designer:	G.O'Brien Kennedy	
Builder:	Estuary Sailboats	
Rig:	bermudan/gunter	
No. of crew:	two	

No. built / registered: 1,150 approx.

Class secretary: David Everett,
89 Newland Mill, Witney, Oxon
OX8 6SZ

First produced in 1965, the **Otter** is a one-design grp dinghy suitable for all crews and capable of high-performance, especially upwind. She is a versatile dinghy with her conventional round-bilged hull, being robust enough for sail training, exciting to race and seaworthy enough for family cruising: she can also be rowed or fitted with an outboard. Normally bermudan rigged, she can be sailed gunter rigged and an optional spinnaker is available for downwind performance. Ashore, she is light and easy to handle and cartoppable.

PACER

PN:1191 (RN)

LOA:	12'6"	3.82m
Beam:	4' 10"	1.47m
Draught:	5"	0.10m
Mast height:	18'8"	5.68m
Sail area:	85sq.ft.	7.89sq.m.
Spinnaker:	80sq.ft.	7.43sq.m.
Weight:	130lb	59kg hull
Construction:	plywood/grp	
Designer:	Jack Holt	
Builder:	Brian Cory (grp), Frank Ward (wooden kits)	
Rig:	bermudan sloop	
No. of crew:	two	

No. built / registered: 2,400

Class secretary: Kate Fitzsimmons, 12, Spring Vale, Greenhithe, Kent DA9 9HA

One-design with spinnaker suitable for amateur construction using the stitch and glue method, which is stable and safe for cruising but lively for racing, planing easily and performing well in strong winds. All boats have blue sails. Ashore, the lightweight hull is easily cartoppable.

PEGASUS

PN: 1078

LOA:	14'6"	4.42m
Beam:	4' 10"	1.47m
Draught:	4'3"	1.30m
	(plate down)	
Mast height:	20'11"	6.38m
Sail area:	137sq.ft.	14.40sq.m.
Spinnaker:	180sq.ft.	16.50sq.m.
Weight:	200lb	90kg
Construction:	wood/grp/composite	
Designer:	Uffa Fox	
Builder:	various	
Rig:	bermudan sloop	
No. of crew:	two	

No. built / registered: 250

Class secretary: Mr A.T. Hayes,
Bradford Court, Bradford on Tone,
Taunton, Somerset TA4 1HQ

One-design planing boat sailed with a single trapeze. Designed by Uffa Fox in 1958 for amateur construction she has a round-bilged hull and a relatively large sail area.

PHANTOM

PN: 1054 (RN)

LOA:	14'6"	4.42m
Beam:	5' 6"	1.64m
Draught:	n/a	
Mast height:	20'	6.10m
Sail area:	105sq.ft.	9.75sq.m.
Spinnaker:	none	
Weight:	134.2lb	61kg
Construction:	wood/grp sandwich	
Designer:	Paul Wright & Brian Taylor	
Builder:	various	
Rig:	una bermudan	
No. of crew:	one	

No. built / registered: 976

Class secretary: Barry Noon,

7 Pendle View, Burnley Road,

Altham, Nr Accrington, Lancs

BB5 5UY

Designed in 1971 as a one-design high-performance singlehander, the **Phantom** has a hard-chine hull with a deep 'V' bow and a flat run aft and planes easily. With her lightweight hull and large rig on a stayed mast she has a high power to weight ratio but is stable and responsive. There is no trapeze or spinnaker and she can carry a wide range of helm weights although with her powerful rig she is most suitable for heavier crew in the weight range of 12-18stone/76-115kg. The **Phantom** is suitable for home construction using the stitch and glue method or can be bought professionally built in grp foam sandwich or wood. This is a strong and developing class.

RAIDER 18

PN: n/a

LOA:	18'3"	5.65m
Beam:	6' 7.5"	2.02m
Draught:	4'3"	0.23m
Mast height:	n/a	
Sail area:	193sq.ft.	17.9sq.m.
Spinnaker:	220sq.ft.	20.4sq.m.
Weight:	1500lb	681.8kg
	(incl. 645lb/293.3kg	
	ballast)	
Construction:	grp	
Designer:	Chris Hawkins	
Builder:	Porter Bros	
Rig:	bermudan sloop	
No. of crew:	one to six	

No built: 45

Class secretary: n/a

Designed in 1994, the **Raider 18** is a safe and stable self-righting family cruising boat with a centreplate, high topsides and a large self-draining cockpit which is also lively and responsive to sail. The boat can be used as a trailer-sailer or can be left on a mooring.

REDWING (NATIONAL)

PN: n/a

LOA:	14'	4.27m
Beam:	5'	1.50m
Draught:	5'6"	1.75m
	(plate down)	
Mast height:	22'	6.90m
Sail area:	145sq.ft.	13.50sq.m.
Spinnaker:	none	
Weight:	275lb	125kg
Construction:	clinker wood	
Designer:	Uffa Fox	
Builder:	Clifford Adams(Looe)	
Rig:	bermudan sloop	
No. of crew:	two	

No. built / registered: 243

Class secretary: Brian P. Carvey,
1 Portbigham, The Quay, West Looe,
Cornwall PL13 2BU

The class was designed in 1938 for the Looe Sailing Club and conditions in Looe Bay as a tougher and stiffer version of the **International 14** (see p.69) and the first boat was built in 1939 and is still sailing today: National status was granted in 1954. The class is one-design built traditionally of clinker wood and half-decked and gives highly competitive racing. There have been a number of developments in the class including the introduction of a wooden centreboard in 1966, trapeze in 1976 and alloy spars in 1984. Many of the oldest boats are still raced competitively and new boats are still being added to the fleet. There are major fleets in the South West and in south west Wales.

ROYAL BURNHAM ONE DESIGN RB

PN: n/a

LOA:	20'	6.10m
Beam:	6' 8"	2.04m
Draught:	3'3"	0.97m
Mast height:	18'	5.49m
Sail area:	240sq.ft.	22.3sq.m.
Spinnaker:	none	
Weight:	n/a	
Construction:	wood	
Designer:	Norman Dallimore	
Builder:	William King & R.Stone	
Rig:	bermudan sloop	
No. of crew	three to five	

No. built / registered: 23

Class secretary: Mrs W Wagstaff, 3 Warners Hall, 70 High Street, Burnham-on-Crouch, CM0 8AA

Commissioned by the Royal Burnham Yacht Club to provide the club with a racing dayboat class, twenty three boats were built in 1932 by two local yards. Twenty one of these original boats are still in commission and a twenty fourth boat is at present under construction. The design is traditional, with a deep displacement hull, wide beam and high freeboard, giving excellent heavy weather characteristics and making the boat ideal for family sailing as well as for racing.

RS 200

PN: n/a

LOA:	13'	4.0m
Beam:	6'	1.83m
Draught:	3'6"	1.10m
Mast height:	n/a	
Sail area:	124sq.ft.	11.52sq.m.
Spinnaker:	89sq.ft.	8.29sq.m.
Weight:	172lb	78kg
Construction:	grp coremat	
Designer:	Phil Morrison	
Builder:	LDC Racing Sailboats	
Rig:	bermudan sloop	
No. of crew:	two	

No. built / registered: new class

Class secretary: Richard George,
37 Boursland Close, Bradley Stoke
North, Bristol, Avon BS12 ODE

Launched in January 1996, the **RS 200** is the smallest dinghy in the RS range and an allround racing boat suitable for the inexperienced and the expert alike.The hull is strong and stiff, the cockpit spacious and the pivoting centreboard and rudder enhance the manoeuvrability of the boat making her stable, responsive and exciting to sail. Rigged with a fully-battened main and jib with an asymmetric spinnaker set on a retractable bowsprit available as an optional extra, she is suitable for an all-up crew weight of 15-21stone/95-134kg. The **RS 200** will appeal to all categories of dinghy sailor and may prove to be a strong rival to established fleets such as the **Enterprise** (see p.53)**, Lark** (see p.88)**, Merlin Rocket** (see p.105) and the **National Twelve** (see p.109).

RS 400

PN: 969 (RN)

LOA:	14'10"	4.52m
Beam:	6'6"	2.0m
Draught:	2'11"	0.90m
Mast height:	21'11"	6.75m
Sail area:	159sq.ft.	14.76sq.m.
Spinnaker:	150sq.ft.	13.94sq.m.
	(asymmetric)	
Weight:	187lb	85kg
Construction:	grp	
Designer:	Phil Morrison	
Builder:	LDC Racing Sailboats	
Rig:	bermudan sloop	
No. of crew:	two	

No. built / registered: 160

Class secretary: Richard George,
37 Boursland Close, Bradley Stoke
North, Bristol BS12 0DE

Launched in 1994, this high quality one-design sitting-out doublehander already has an established reputation and has been selected for the UK Dinghy Sailing National Championships. The **RS 400** is fast and manoeuvrable yet easily handled. The hull is lightweight yet stiff and strong with flared topsides, the interior layout simple yet efficient and the pivoting rudder and centreboard make launching easy and shallow-water sailing no problem. The rig of fully-battened main, jib and asymmetric spinnaker has a high aspect ratio and the asymmetric spinnaker can be "rocked" to windward to allow the dinghy to achieve very fast downwind speeds.

RS 600

PN: 920 (RN)

LOA:	14'8"	4.47m
Beam:	6' 4"	1.93m
(with wings)	7'0"	2.13m
Draught:	n/a	
Mast height:	n/a	
Sail area:	131sq.ft.	12.14sq.m.
Spinnaker:	none	
Weight:	115lb	52kg
Construction:	grp sandwich	
Designer:	Clive Everest & Nick Peters	
Builder:	LDC Racing Sailboats	
Rig:	una bermudan	
No. of crew:	one	

No. built / registered: 150

Class secretary: Graham Simmonds
26A Craignish Avenue, Norbury,
London SW16 4RN

Launched in January 1994, this one-design singlehander class with una rig on a stayed rotating mast and trapeze is claimed to be the fastest singlehanded production monohull dinghy in the world. The hull and rig are very light but strong and the wings are available in two different widths and weights giving a wide competitive weight range. The fully-battened sail can be easily reefed giving a reduction of 20% which makes sailing the dinghy within the reach of most competent dinghy sailors.

SALCOMBE YAWL

PN: 1135 (RN)

LOA:	16'	4.88m
Beam:	7' 7"	2.13m
Draught:	variable	
Mast height:	25'	7.47m
Sail area:	175sq.ft.	16.24sq.m.
Spinnaker:	none	
Weight:	838lb	381kg min.
Construction:	clinker wood	
Designer:	several including	
	Morgan Giles	
Builder:	various	
Rig:	bermudan yawl	
No. of crew:	two/three	

No. built / registered: 160

Class secretary: Nick Walker,
The Old Workhouse, Union Road,
Kingsbridge, Devon

One of the oldest racing keelboat classes, an "envelope" of measurement rules was first established in the 1940s and these have recently been updated twice to prevent outrageous development.

SCORPION

PN: 1069 (SY)

LOA:	14'	4.27m
Beam:	4' 10"	1.45m
Draught:	3'6"	1.04m
Mast height:	20'	6.10m
Sail area:	107sq.ft.	9.94sq.m.
Spinnaker:	120sq.ft.	11.15sq.m.
Weight:	178.5lb	81kg
Construction:	ply/grp	
Designer:	Taprell Dorling	

Builder: Duffin Boats, Derek Jolly Boats, Gosling Dinghycraft, Paintcraft, Rowsell & Morrison

Rig: bermudan sloop

No. of crew: two

No. built / registered: 1,945

Class secretary: William Jeffcoate, Church Farm, Edingley, Notts NG22 8BE

A high-performance two person racing dinghy sailed without a trapeze and with a powerful rig which gives exciting sailing in all weathers. Designed in 1960 to be launched and recovered through the Cornish surf, this one-design class has a lightweight hard-chine planing hull with large integral buoyancy tanks and pivoting centreboard. Rig controls and cockpit layout can be varied and much development has taken place recently in this area making the **Scorpion** a highly competitive boat suitable for a range of crew weights while the easily adjusted rig enables her to be sailed in all weathers. She has terrific acceleration, is responsive, points well and tacks very easily and has a reputation for carrying her spinnaker on a tight reach. Ashore, the lightweight hull is easily handled.

SEANFLY

PN: 1074 (RN)

LOA:	14'9"	4.49m
Beam:	5' 9"	1.75m
Draught:	3'10"	1.17m
Mast height:	21'6"	6.55m
Sail area:	120sq.ft.	11.14sq.m.
Spinnaker:	135sq.ft.	12.54sq.m.
Weight:	240lb	109kg all up
Construction:	ply/grp	
Designer:	Stan Herbert & J.Kelley	
Builder:	C.M.Marine, Bob Hoare & amateur	
Rig:	bermudan sloop	
No. of crew:	two/three	

No. built / registered: 654

Class secretary: M.J.Appleby,
1 Willow Close, Crawley, Sussex
RH10 2HT

One-design dinghy developed by Stan Herbert from an original design by J. Kelley which is a larger form of the **Mayfly** (see p.179) with a deep v form hull and swept-up chine built in marine ply or grp with plywood decks. The **Seafly** is a fast non-trapeze dinghy which is sailed with a spinnaker: she is roomy and light to handle yet stiff, performing well as a racer and a cruiser especially in rough wind and sea conditions.

The class association is currently negotiating to acquire the copyright of the design in order to appoint new class builders.

12 SQUARE METRE SHARPIE

PN: 1027 (RN)

LOA:	19'8"	5.99m
Beam:	4' 8"	1.43m
Draught:	6.25"	0.16m
Mast height:	15'11"	4.85m
Sail area:	129sq.ft.	12.0 sq.m.
	min	
Spinnaker:	none	
Weight:	507lb	230kg min
Construction:	carvel wood	
Designer:	J. Kroeger	
Builder:	various	
Rig:	gunter sloop	
No. of crew:	two	

No. built / registered: 135

Class secretary: Mrs Cherry Case
Hayhow Barn, Standard Road,
Wells-next-the-Sea, Norfolk,
NR23 1JX

One-design from 1931 with long narrow half-decked hard-chine carvel mahogany hull, daggerboard and wishbone tiller. The rig is a high-peaked gunter mainsail with a large overlapping staysail with a minimum overall area of 12 sq.m. In 1933 the class gained International status and in 1956 was selected for the Olympic Games. The class is still actively raced at several venues in Norfolk and at Langstone in Chichester Harbour with several of the original boats, built by Abeking and Rasmussen still competing. Approximately sixty boats are still in racing condition.

SIGNET

PN: 1268 (RN)

LOA:	12'6"	3.80m
Beam:	4' 9"	1.45m
Draught:	5"	0.13m
Mast height:	18'6"	5.63m
Sail area:	105sq.ft.	9.70sq.m.
Spinnaker:	90sq.ft.	8.30sq.m.
Weight:	160lb	73kg hull
Construction:	marine ply	
Designer:	Ian Proctor	
Builder:	Ron Beasley	
Rig:	bermudan sloop	
No. of crew:	two	

No. built / registered: 908

Class secretary: Mrs Joyce Cowern, Brindley, Giggetty Lane, Wombourne South Staffs WV5 0AY

A lightweight multi-purpose dinghy designed in 1961 and sponsored by the *'Sunday Times'* for easy home construction from scratch with full scale plans. The **Signet** moves well in light airs and planes easily: she is stable and has built-in buoyancy and is suitable for both beginners and the more experienced sailor. The spacious and uncluttered cockpit can carry three or four for cruising or two for racing.

SKUA

PN: n/a

LOA:	17'0"	5.18m
Beam:	5' 2"	1.57m
Draught:	2'9"	0.13m
Mast height:	n/a	
Sail area:	140sq.ft.	13.0sq.m.
Spinnaker:	120sq.ft.	11.15sq.m.
Weight:	260lb	120kg hull
Construction:	marine ply	
Designer:	Jack Robertson	
Builder:	amateur	
Rig:	bermudan sloop	
No. of crew:	two	

No. built / registered: 56 in UK

Class secretary: David Lumbard,
8 Kirk Ports, North Berwick,
East Lothian EH39 4HL

One-design drop-keel boat designed for hard weather estuary sailing in the Firth of Forth and first launched at the Royal Forth Yacht Club in 1964. The **Skua** combines the planing performance of a racing dinghy with the safety factor of a fin and bulb keelboat. The relatively small sail area is well distributed between the main and the genoa to facilitate hard weather handling and the hull shape is easily driven. The hard-chine hull was designed for home construction but grp kits or complete boats are also available. The class is mainly sailed at Edinburgh and North Berwick.

SNIPE (INTERNATIONAL)

PN: 1117 (RN)

LOA:	15'6"	4.72m
Beam:	5'	1.52m
Draught:	3'3"	1.0m
	(plate down)	
Mast height:	20'1"	6.12m
Sail area:	128sq.ft.	11.90sq.m.
Spinnaker:	none	
Weight:	275b	125kg hull
Construction:	grp/wood/composite	
Designer:	W.Crosby (USA)	
Builder:	Itsa Marine, W.Cowes	
Rig:	bermudan sloop	
No. of crew:	two	

No. built / registered: 29,026   world-
                                              wide

Class secretary:John B. Love,
8 Pasture Drive, Croft, Warrington,
Cheshire WA3 7LH

Strict one-design hard-chine racing dinghy first designed in 1931: the first fleet in the U.K. was established at Dover in 1933 and by 1936, the **Snipe** class was the World's largest racing class. International status was granted in 1958 and the class is now sailed in over 20 countries with 216 racing fleets, 9 of which are in the UK. The construction of the hull is sturdy with a minimum weight which ensures a long competitive life and non-sensitivity to crew weight and which enables the **Snipe** to race safely and efficiently in strong winds without the need for trapezes, racks etc. There is some laxity in cockpit layout, most of which are self-draining. Spinnakers are not allowed but an extra long whisker pole (8'8"/2.6m) enables the jib to be goose-winged forward of the bow. Racing the **Snipe** requires skill and tactics, rather than great physical input.

SOLING (INTERNATIONAL)

PN: 914 (RN)

LOA:	26'10"	8.20m
Beam:	6' 3"	1.90m
Draught:	4'3"	1.30m
Mast height:	30'6"	9.30m
Sail area:	233.7sq.ft.	
	21.7sq.m.	
Spinnaker:	variable	
Weight:	2277lb	1035kg
	(incl. keel)	
Construction:	grp	
Designer:	Jan Linge (Denmark)	
Builder:	Abbott (Canada)	
	Borresens (Denmark)	
Rig:	bermudan sloop	
No. of crew:	three	

No. built / registered: 162 (UK only)

Class secretary: Mrs D Reed,
P.O.Box 2, Bordon, Hants GU35 9JX

Three-man performance keelboat with a fractional rig and variable size spinnaker designed in 1964. Chosen as an Olympic class in 1972, she is the largest Olympic sailing class but can be sailed by sailors of all ages and weights (average all-up crew weight 40stone/255kg).

SOLO (NATIONAL)

PN: 1155 (PY)

LOA:	12'5"	3.78m
Beam:	5'1"	1.55m
Draught:	3'5"	1.04m
	(plate down)	
Mast height:	20'	6.10m
Sail area:	90sq.ft.	8.36sq.m.
Spinnaker:	none	
Weight:	155lb	70kg
Construction:	wood/grp/composite	
Designer:	Jack Holt	
Builder:	various	
Rig:	una bermudan	
No. of crew:	one	

No. built / registered: 4,096

Class secretary: R.N.Crawshaw,
14 Devonshire Drive, Camberley,
Surrey GU15 3UB

Designed in 1956 and sponsored by 'Yachting World', the **Solo** is a one-design high-performance singlehander with a distinctive large fully-battened mainsail on a stayed mast which can be controlled to suit the helm's weight and preference.The hull is double-chine with flared side decks and can be built from plans or bought part-finished or completed. Class rules allow changes in materials and methods of construction to keep the boat up to date.

SPLASH

PN: n/a

LOA:	11'7.8"	3.55m
Beam:	4' 3.3"	1.30m
Draught:	2'4.3"	0.72m
Mast height:	17'	3.78m
Sail area:	59 sq.ft.	5.50sq.m.
Spinnaker:	none	
Weight:	107.8lb	49kg
Construction:	grp sandwich	
Designer:	Jac de Ridder	
Builder:	Moores of Wroxham	
Rig:	una bermudan	
No. of crew:	one	

No. built / registered: 800

Class secretary: Mr R. Goodison,
40 Fullerton Drive, Brinsworth,
Rotherham, S. Yorks S60 5MQ

A new (1990) strict one-design singlehander, established in Holland as a youth class and fast becoming so in the UK. With a simple but easily adjusted rig and a roomy cockpit with a comfortable sitting-out position, the **Splash** is ideal for youth sailors to develop their skills and can also be enjoyed by all the family. She sails well without needing great weight or strength suiting weights of 7.5-9.5stone/50-60kg unlike many other larger singlehanders. Ashore, she is easily handled and is cartoppable.

SPORT 14

PN: n/a

LOA:	14'7"	4.45m
Beam:	5' 10"	1.80m
Draught:	n/a	
Mast height:	n/a	
Sail area:	118sq.ft.	11.0sq.m.
Spinnaker:	183sq.ft.	17.0sq.m.
Weight:	264lb	120kg hull
Construction:	grp sandwich	
Designer:	Ian Howlett	
Builder:	Topper International	
Rig:	bermudan sloop	
No. of crew:	two/four	
No. built / registered: 35 (new class)		
Class secretary: none yet		

A new high-performance sit-in racer with asymmetric spinnaker. Designed as a family club racer, the **Sport 14** has a powerful and beamy hull and is stable, comfortable, fast and easily handled: the cockpit has a relatively high freeboard and is self-draining. The main is fully-battened and the asymmetric spinnaker is set on a through-hull pole.

SQUIB (NATIONAL)

PY:1107

LOA:	19'0"	5.79m
Beam:	6' 2"	1.87m
Draught:	3'3"	0.91m
Mast height:	variable	
Sail area:	173sq.ft.	15.0sq.m.
Spinnaker:	145sq.ft.	13.5sq.m.
Weight:	1,500lb	682kg
Construction:	grp	
Designer:	Oliver Lee	
Builder:	Barker Brewer Boats	
Rig:	bermudan sloop	
No. of crew:	two	

No. built / registered: over 760

Class secretary: Celia Bennett,
60 The Avenue, Leighton Bromswold,
Huntingdon, Cambs, PE18 OSH

Half-decked two-man keelboat designed in 1968 as an inexpensive general-purpose one-design class suitable for club racing and family cruising, the **Squib** was granted National status in 1972. She is strongly constructed with a round bottom and fin keel and has a high ballast ratio and built-in buoyancy which makes her stable and powerful and able to carry full sail in a strong wind but she also performs well in light airs. Good sea-keeping qualities make her particularly suitable for coastal and estuary waters and the foredeck rises around the mast to give her a small cuddy. There are 24 active racing fleets in the UK. Ashore, the **Squib** can be easily trailed.

STREAKER

PN :1167 (SY)

LOA:	12'9"	3.89m
Beam:	4' 9"	1.44m
Draught:	n/a	
Mast height:	21'	6.30m
Sail area:	70sq.ft.	6.50sq.m.
Spinnaker:	none	
Weight:	105lb	48kg hull
Construction:	grp/wood/composite	
Designer:	Jack Holt (1975)	
Builder:	Jack Holt Ltd. & Brian	
	Cory Boatbuilders Ltd.	
Rig:	una bermudan	
No. of crew:	one	

No. built / registered: 1,478

Class secretary:Vernon Penketh,
31 Oak Tree Close, Strensall, York
YO3 5TE

A one-design singlehander with a stayed una rig suitable for the average helm which is light and responsive on the helm and planes fast. Originally designed for home construction, this is a well-proven class with close racing throughout the fleet. The large cockpit has a central thwart and room for two when cruising. Ashore, the **Streaker** is light and easy to handle and cartoppable.

SUNBEAM

PN: n/a

LOA:	26'5"	8.05m
Beam:	6'	1.83m
Draught:	3'9"	1.14m
Mast height:	32'6"	9.90m
Sail area:	300sq.ft.	27.87sq.m.
Spinnaker:	155sq.ft.	14.40sq.m.
Weight:	approx. 3 tons hull	
Construction:	wood	
Designer:	Alfred Westmacott	
Builder:	Woodnutt & Co. Ltd	
	and others	
Rig:	fractional bermudan	
No. of crew:	two/three	

No. built / registered: 44

Class secretary: Alan Stannah,
Freshfields, Sandy Lane, East Ashling,
Chichester PO18 9AT

Built in 1923 to form a new class on the River Hamble, this one-design wooden keelboat is a timeless classic with her long ends and large sail area, and is considered by many to be Alfred Westmacott's masterpiece. All the original 39 boats were built at Woodnutt & Co's yard at St Helens on the Isle of Wight of carvel pitch pine planking on American elm bent timbers. All but one of these original boats are still sailing and racing today together with five new boats and the class has the longest unbroken record of attendance at Cowes Week. The class is restricted, allowing variations in rigging and distribution of sail area within limits.The class is based in two areas; at Itchenor in Chichester Harbour (the 'Solent Sunbeams') and at Falmouth with the distinction that at Itchenor, boats are sailed with a spinnaker whilst at Falmouth the headsail is still boomed out following the original 1922 sail plan. All Sunbeams have a name ending in 'y'.

SUPERNOVA

PN: n/a

LOA:	14'5"	4.42m
Beam:	4' 11"	1.50m
Draught:	3'3"	1.0m
Mast height:	18'5"	5.60m
Sail area:	86.2sq.ft.	8.0sq.m.
Spinnaker:	none	
Weight:	137.5lb	62.5kg
Construction:	grp	
Designer:	Mark Giles	
Builder:	Giles Reinforced	
	Plastics Ltd	
Rig:	una bermudan	
No. of crew:	one	

No. built / registered: 13 (new class)

Class secretary: n/a

A new one-design high-performance singlehander with a large self-draining cockpit and high boom suitable for average or larger sailors when racing which can accommodate two when cruising.The lightweight hull has no wings or trapeze and the rig is a fully-battened Mylar sail on a sealed, stayed mast. The **Supernova** will give more speed than the traditional sit-out one-designs without a trapeze, sliding seat or wings.

SWALLOW

S

PN: n/a

LOA:	25'6"	7.79m
Beam:	5' 8"	1.73m
Draught:	3'6"	1.05m
Mast height:	30'	9.0m
Sail area:	200sq.ft.	18.50sq.m.
Spinnaker:	215sq.ft.	20.0sq.m.
Weight:	2250lb	1022kg
Construction:	wood or grp	
Designer:	Tom Thorneycroft	
Builder:	various	
Rig:	bermudan sloop	
No. of crew:	three	

No. built / registered: 89

Class secretary: Mrs M. L. Clarke,
20, Montana Road, London,
SW20 8TW

Strict one-design keelboat designed in 1946 and used in the 1948 Olympic Games when Stewart Morris won the Gold Medal. With her sleek hull, high-aspect ratio rig and big spinnaker she feels like a dinghy to sail but with the stability of a keelboat. The **Swallow** provides close and exciting racing and planes easily on a broad reach, and is ideal for harbour or open sea sailing. The fleet is centred at Itchenor in Chichester Harbour and is about 25 stong. Originally built in wood, new hulls are now grp following a change in class rules.

SWORDFISH (NATIONAL)

PN: 1117 (RN)

LOA:	15'	4.57m
Beam:	5'	1.54m
Draught:	9"/4'9"	0.23/1.45m
Mast height:	22'	6.71m
Sail area:	130sq.ft.	12.0sq.m.
Spinnaker:	80sq.ft.	7.43sq.m.
Weight:	375lb	170kg
Construction:	hot-moulded plywood	
Designer:	Uffa Fox	
Builder:	Fairey Marine	
Rig:	fractional bermudan	
No. of crew:	two or three	

No. built / registered: 219

Class secretary: B Weston,

18 Schofield Drive, Darfield, Barnsley,

South Yorkshire S73 9AX

Half-decked family cruiser/racer designed in 1946 as the 15' National Class and built by Fairey Marine: the round-bottomed hull and layout are similar to that of the **Firefly** (see p.59). Deemed uneconomic, the last **Swordfish** was built in 1963, but the hull moulds were used to build the **Albacore** (see p.21) which has a larger sail area.

TASAR

PN: 1021 (SY)

LOA:	14'10"	4.52m
Beam:	5' 9"	1.75m
Draught:	4'6"	1.40m
	(plate down)	
Mast height:	n/a	
Sail area:	123sq.ft.	11.43sq.m.
Spinnaker:	none	
Weight:	150lb	68kg
Construction:	grp foam sandwich	
Designer:	Frank Bethwaite	
Builder:	Rondar	
Rig:	bermudan sloop	
No. of crew:	two	

No. built / registered: 2,650

Class secretary: John Rischmiller,
83 Waverley Drive, Chertsey,
Surrey KT16 9PF

Two-man one-design racing dinghy designed in 1975 particularly to appeal to husband and wife crews. The rig is a fully-battened main on a rotating wing mast and the hull is lightweight and planes easily. Class rules require compensating weights to be carried if the combined crew weight is less than 20.4stone/130kg. The class is sailed at over 30 clubs in the U.K. Ashore, the **Tasar** is easily handled and cartoppable.

TEMPEST (INTERNATIONAL)

PN: 937 (RN)

LOA:	22'	6.70m
Beam:	6' 6"	1.97m
Draught:	3'7"	1.10m
Mast height:	29'2"	8.90m
Sail area:	247sq.ft.	23sq.m
Spinnaker:	225sq.ft.	21sq.m
Weight:	1034lb	470kg all up

Construction: grp

Designer: Ian Proctor (1963)

Builder: Mader, Germany

Rig: fractional bermudan sloop

No. of crew: two

No. built / registered: 110 (UK)

Class secretary: R. J. Robinson, Rose Cottage, Thomas Close, Calthwaite, Penrith, CA11 9QF

Two-man keelboat sailed with a trapeze especially in Europe. The **Tempest** sailed as an Olympic Class in 1976 when it briefly replaced the **Star** (see p.181). A new deck moulding is now in production.

TIDEWAY

PN: 1447 (RN)

LOA:	12'	3.66m
Beam:	5'	1.52m
Draught:	3'	0.91m
Mast height:	18'	5.49m
gunter	12'6"	3.80m
Sail area:	81sq.ft.	7.52sq.m.
Spinnaker:	none	
Weight:	240lb	109kg hull
Construction:	clinker wood/grp	
Designer:	Lew Walker	
Builder:	L.H.Walker (1954-79)	
	Tepco Boats(1991)	
Rig:	bermudan or sliding gunter	
No. of crew:	two/three	

No. built / registered: 550

Class secretary: Mary Davies,
70 Holland St, Ebbw Vale NP3 6HY

A restricted class of traditional clinker-built dinghies first built in 1954 when they were known as the **Walker 12**, and renamed the **Tideway** in 1963. New boats are now being constructed in grp simulated clinker. The **Tideway** is a stable and seaworthy boat which is sturdily constructed and suitable for family day-sailing, cruising and racing. Boats can be open or with a fore-deck, side decks and slatted side benches.The sliding gunter rig is most common although some boats are bermudan rigged: with the former, the spars will fit inside the boat for ease of transport.

The **Tepco Tideway 14** is a larger version, based on the **Walker Family 14**, 14'2"/4.3m LOA, with a 5'10"/1.6m Beam and a Sail Area of 106sq.ft./9.8sq.m. and is also built in grp simulated clinker.

TINKER TRAVELLER

PN: n/a

LOA:	12'	3.66m
Beam:	4' 9"	1.45m
Draught:	2'10"	0.86m
Mast height:	16'	4.88m
Sail area:	58sq.ft.	5.39sq.m
(masthead jib)	74sq.ft.	6.87sq.m.
Spinnaker:	none	
Weight:	70lb	32kg hull
Construction:	hypalon- inflatable	
Designer:	F. Benyon-Tinker / J. Henshaw	
Builder:	Henshaw Inflatables	
Rig:	bermudan sloop	
No. of crew:	one to three	

No. built / registered: 3,150

Class secretary: John K.Cruise, Woodhayes, Burton Row, Brent Knoll, Highbridge, Somerset TA9 4BW

A versatile inflatable dinghy, often used as a yacht tender/liferaft, which is sturdy and stable and performs well under sail, power or oars. The **Tinker Traveller** is also raced and performs as well as a **Mirror** (see p.107): the **Star Traveller** has a masthead jib. The **Tinker Tramp** is a smaller version of this dinghy, 9'/2.57m LOA with a sail area of 51sq.ft./4.74sq m. or 64sq.ft./5.95sq.m. in the **Super Tramp** version with a masthead jib. Over 3,000 have been built.

The **Tinker Funsail** is the newest in the range, 10'3"/3.15m LOA, 4'11"/1.5m wide with a sail area of 41sq.ft/3.8sq.m. So far, 120 of these have been built.

TOPPER (INTERNATIONAL)

PN: 1288 (PY)

LOA:	11'2"	3.4m
Beam:	3' 10"	1.2m
Draught:	3"/2'6"	0.08/0.8m
	(plate up/down)	
Mast height:	17'6"	5.40m
Sail area:	56sq.ft.	5.2sq.m.
Spinnaker:	none	
Weight:	95lb	43kg
Construction:	polypropylene	
Designer:	Ian Proctor (1976)	
Builder:	Topper International	
Rig:	una bermudan	
No. of crew:	one	

No. built / registered: 40,100

Class secretary: Helen Evans,
120 Main Road, Shavington, Crewe,
Cheshire CW2 5EE

A simple, lightweight strict one-design dinghy built of polpropylene which is virtually unbreakable and unsinkable. The rig is a luff-sleeved loose-footed and unbattened sail which slides on to an unstayed mast and which is fully reefable. Easy to sail for the inexperienced with its modest sail area, a well-sailed **Topper** provides exhilarating performance, especially in moderate to heavy winds when it is quick to plane. With a low freeboard and scow bow, the **Topper** is wet to sail but ideal for juniors and lighter adults of 8-11stone/51-70kg and with plenty of room in an uncluttered cockpit for two. One of the most popular dinghies, especially with sailing clubs and schools, there is a huge racing circuit, the identical hulls ensuring evenly matched racing. Ashore, the **Topper** is easily handled and cartoppable and boats have a high resale value.

TOY

PN: 1012 (RN)

LOA:	15'	4.57m
Beam:	4' 3"	1.29m
Draught:	4"/3'6"	0.1/1.09m
	(plate up/down)	
Mast height:	19'10"	6.05m
Sail area:	110sq.ft.	10.22sq.m.
Spinnaker:	none	
Weight:	143lb	65kg hull
Construction:	grp	
Designer:	Tony Allen	
Builder:	various	
Rig:	una bermudan	
No. of crew:	one	

No. built / registered: 224

Class secretary:

Kelvin Morton, 5

Minsmere Drive, Clacton

Essex CO16 8AD

High-performance singlehanded racing dinghy with sliding seat which extends 3'3"/1m to windward when in use. The **Toy** was designed in 1964 as the result of a '*Yachting World*' design competition, and is sometimes used as an introduction to the **International Canoe** (see p.81). Ideal crew weight is 10-12.5stone/64-80kg.

Could all current owners please contact the class secretary who is keen to trace the whereabouts of all existing boats.

VICTORY

Z

PN: n/a

LOA:	20'9"	6.34m
Beam:	5' 10"	1.79m
Draught:	2'6"	0.76m
Mast height:	26'9"	8.17m
Sail area:	200sq.ft.	18.6sq.m.
Spinnaker:	200sq.ft.	18.6sq.m.
Weight:	1.5 tons all up	
Construction:	clinker wood	
Designer:	A. Westmacott	
Builder:	Feltham, Hampers	
	Perry, Woodnutts	
Rig:	bermudan sloop	
No. of crew:	three	

No. built / registered: n/a

Class secretary: Miss D.M.Freeman, Top Flat, 11 Auckland Road West, Southsea PO4 ORG

Developed from a 1904 design for the Bembridge Class by Alfred Westmacott, the **Victory** class was established in 1934. She has two distinguishing features, the clinker hull and the black finish. Although never as popular as the **XOD** class (see p.153), this keelboat, with her short ends and half-heart shaped rudder is still popular in Portsmouth Harbour, with 25-30 boats racing annually at Cowes. With her long keel and lots of ballast she is heavy and not at her best in light weather, performing well however, in boisterous conditions.

WANDERER

PN: 1129

LOA:	14'	4.27m
Beam:	5' 10"	1.78m
Draught:	3'6"	1.09m
	(plate down)	
Mast height:	22'	6.3m
Sail area:	115sq.ft.	10.68sq.m.
Spinnaker:	107sq.ft.	9.90sq.m.
Weight:	285lb	129kg
Construction:	grp	
Designer:	Ian Proctor	
Builder:	Anglo Marine	
	Services Ltd.	
Rig:	bermudan sloop	
No. of crew:	two/four	

No. built / registered: 1,302

Class secretary: Stan Telling,

75 Elers Road, London W13 9QB

Strict one-design boat designed in 1984, and at 14' LOA, a lighter and smaller sister to the **Wayfarer** (see p.151), suitable for family day-sailing, cruising and racing. There is a choice of sails for racing or cruising.The **Wanderer** is robust, safe and versatile, with a roomy cockpit large enough to allow two adults to camp, sleeping one either side of the centreplate and is available with a wood or steel centreplate. Ashore, she is relatively light and easy to handle and rig and can be easily trailed. The class is used by many sailing establishments.

WAYFARER

PN: 1099 (PY)

LOA:	15'10"	4.82m
Beam:	6' 1"	1.85m
Draught:	3'10"	1.16m
	(plate down)	
Mast height:	22'4"	6.80m
Sail area:	141sq.ft.	13.1sq.m.
Spinnaker:	145sq.ft.	13.5sq.m.
Weight:	372lb	167kg hull
Construction:	wood/grp/composite	
Designer:	Ian Proctor (1957)	
Builder:	Moores of Wroxham	
	& Porter Brothers	
Rig:	bermudan sloop	
No. of crew:	one to five (2 racing)	

No. built / registered: 9,730

Class secretary:Diane Aps,
Milestone House, Main Street,
Middleton, Market Harborough,
Leics LE16 8YU

Classic all-rounder family boat, the **Wayfarer** is a proven sea-kindly boat used for training, cruising and racing and is comfortable and dry.The class has been cruised as far afield as Scandinavia, the Mediterranean and even across the Atlantic: the adventures of Frank and Margaret Dye in their boat are well known. With built-in buoyancy she is a very stable boat and difficult to capsize and lies safely on a mooring. Different versions of the boat are available for cruising and racing, the former having a built in bulkhead, watertight storage areas and a self-draining cockpit. There is intense competition within the racing fleet. Ashore, the boat is heavy and rather more difficult to manouevre than many other dinghies. The **Wayfarer** holds her price well.

WINEGLASS

PN: 1079 (RN)

LOA:	15'	4.57m
Beam:	5' 10"	1.77m
Draught:	3'6"	1.06m
Mast height:	22'	6.7m
Sail area:	123sq.ft.	11.4sq.m.
Spinnaker:	none	
Weight:	240lb	108.8kg
Construction:	foam sandwich	
Designer:	Trevor Kirby	
Builder:	Don Marine	
Rig:	bermudan sloop	
No. of crew:	two/four	

No. built / registered: 507

Class secretary: John Blair,

73 Church Road, Quarndon, Derby

DE22 5JA

Designed in 1957, as a family cruiser and racer the **Wineglass** is a one-design which is easy to sail and roomy with her uncluttered cockpit and high boom. Her round-bottomed hull has a pronounced flair, making her a good sea-boat. She performs well, particularly in light airs and recently the use of an asymmetric spinnaker has been permitted. Ashore, she is relatively light and easily manoueuvred.

X BOAT

PN rating: n/a

LOA:	20'9"	6.31m
Beam:	6'	1.83m
Draught:	2'9"	0.85m
Mast height:	26'4"	8.02m
Sail area:	275sq.ft.	25.50sq.m.
Spinnaker:	140sq.ft.	13.0sq.m.
Weight:	2875lb	1307kg
	(all up with keel)	
Construction:	clinker wood	
Designer:	A.Westmacott	
Builder:	Clare Lallow, Cowes	
	& others	
Rig:	bermudan sloop	
No. of crew:	three	

No. built / registered: 194

Class secretary: Mrs P Rayner,
Trenance, 29 Wyatts Lane, Cowes
Isle of Wight PO31 8QB

Classic Solent one-design half-decked wooden keelboat class. Boat no1 was built in 1908 and boat no194 was built to the same design in 1994. Introduced by The Motor Yacht Club in 1909, boats were carvel built of pitch pine (later mahogany) with iron keels by Woodnutts and gaff-rigged. After 1928 the bermudan rig was introduced and in 1950, the size of the mainsail was reduced by using a shorter boom thus permitting a standing backstay instead of runners and the size of the foresail was increased. **X Boats** are known as durable and seaworthy boats which are sturdily constructed. The class is enthusiastically raced with strong fleets at Lymington, Itchenor, Parkstone, Cowes, Yarmouth and Hamble, normally turning out 78+ boats for Cowes Week, and thus having the largest class entry.

YACHTING WORLD DAYBOAT

DB

PN: 1199 (RN)

LOA:	14'1"	4.29m max.
Beam:	5' 9"	1.75m max.
Draught:	4'0"	1.22m
		(centreboard down)
Mast height:	20'6"	6.25m max.
Sail area:	138sq.ft.	12.87sq.m.
Spinnaker:	56sq.ft.	5.20sq.m.
Weight:	450lb	204.12kg
Construction:	clinker wood or grp	
Designer:	G. O'Brien Kennedy	
Builder:	Porter Bros.(grp)	
Rig:	bermudan sloop	
No. of crew:	two/three	

No. built / registered: 647

Class secretary: Fiona S. Rainback,
1 Ashmore Crescent, Poole, Dorset,
BH15 4DG

Designed in 1949 for 'Yachting World' magazine as a robust, stable round-bilged dinghy with a generous freeboard suitable for family sailing especially in the open sea. The plans were originally available only to amateur builders but in 1955, professional building under licence was allowed. Although heavily constructed and not originally intended for racing, the **Dayboat** will plane and is raced competitively in a number of fleets around the country: she has particularly good windward performance in rough water. Although a spinnaker can be used for cruising, the rules do not allow it to be carried when racing. Class rules give safety a high priority and each boat must carry sufficient buoyancy, oars and rowlocks, anchor and warp. Ashore, the **Dayboat** can be easily trailed by the average car, although most boats are kept afloat.

YEOMAN

PN: 1107 (PY)

LOA:	20'	6.10m
Beam:	6' 6"	1.98m
Draught:	3'2"	0.97m
	(plate down)	
Mast height:	n/a	
Sail area:	192sq.ft.	17.84sq.m.
Spinnaker:	265sq.ft.	24.60sq.m.
Weight:	1395lb	634kg
Construction:	grp	
Designer:	Landamore (1968)	
Builder:	Moores of Wroxham	
Rig:	bermudan	
No. of crew:	two/three	

No. built / registered: 207

Class secretary: Peter Hinton,

7 Launceston Road, Perivale,

Middlesex UB6 7EX

Well-proven keelboat with a sleek hull and cuddy on the fordeck designed both for cruising and racing. The roomy and uncluttered cockpit will accommodate the whole family and the boat can be successfully sailed by crews with all levels of experience.

The **Kinsman** is built to the same specification as the Yeoman, the only difference being the provision of a retractable iron keel which is raised and lowered by a winch, thus enabling the boat to sail in shallow waters and to be left on a drying mooring.

ZEPHYR

PN:n/a

LOA:	8'6"	2.6m
Beam:	4'	1.22m
Draught:	0'3"	0.75m
Mast height:	12'	3.6m
Sail area:	29sq.ft.	2.7sq.m.
Spinnaker:	none	
Weight:	77lb	35kg
Construction:	aluminium	
Designer:	Hugh Welbourn	
Builder:	Zephyr Sailboats	
Rig:	trapezoid/bermudan	
No. of crew:	one/two	

No. built / registered: over 100

Class secretary: Jerry Nuttall,
132 Sheffield Road, Drunfield,
Sheffield S18 6GE

Small, simple lightweight aluminium-hulled dinghy with an inner glassfibre moulding providing side buoyancy tanks, thwart and a floor doubler. The **Zephyr** is available in several different versions and is suitable for use as a tender. She is easy to rig, and sails well with a high boom, lifting rudder and a reefing sail and is easy to control. For sailing, a choice of rigs is available: the trapezoid rig on a bent aluminium mast provides a better performance but makes stowage more difficult while the bermudan rig is easier to manage. The **Zephyr** is popular as a youth training dinghy and is raced as a one-design class. The hull is virtually indestructible and maintenance free and most dents can simply be hammered out.

CATAPULT

PN: 871 (RN)

LOA:	16'5"	5.0m
Beam:	7' 5"	2.25m
Draught:	1'6"	0.45m
Mast height:	23'7"	7.20m
Sail area:	108sq.ft.	10.0sq.m.
Spinnaker:	none	
Weight:	180lb only	81kg hull
Construction:	aluminium frame & inflatable hulls	
Designer:	Jon Montgomery	
Builder:	Topper International	
Rig:	una with wishbone boom	

No. of crew: one/two

No. built / registered: 800

Class secretary: J.Peperell,

23 Heatham Park,Twickenham

TW2 7S

Designed in 1981, this is a high-performance catamaran for the solo sailor to race or for sailing two-up. The **Catapult** has inflatable hypalon hulls, making her light, manoeuvreable, stable and easy to handle pointing high and tacking easily, unlike many una-rigged catamarans, and there is an optional single trapeze and jib. The **Catapult** is light and easily launched and can be totally dismantled for transportation and storage, making this the ideal craft for the town dweller.

CHALLENGER MARK 111

PN: n/a

LOA:	15'	4.57m
Beam:	11' 6"	3.50m
Draught:	1'6"	0.45m
	(plate down)	
Mast height:	21'4"	6.50m
Sail area:	106sq.ft.	9.89sq.m.
Spinnaker:	none	
Weight:	262lb	119kg
	(hull & sponsons)	
Construction:	grp	
Designer:	Roderick Macalpine-Downie	
Builder:	Anglo Marine	
Rig:	aerorig/bermudan	
No. of crew:	two	

No. built / registered: 174

Class secretary: D.Prentice,
23 Mortimer Road, Market Drayton
TF9 2EP

One-design trimaran designed in 1980 as a fast but stable boat for use by both able-bodied and disabled people.There are two versions: the **Mark 11** is a singlehander with a single fully-battened sail (85sq.ft./7.9sq.m.) on a rotating mast while in the **Mark 111**, which has either an aerorig or a full bermudan rig including a jib or optional genoa, the cockpit has been extended to accommodate a crew sitting in front of the helmsman. The hull is double-skinned with built in buoyancy tanks and outstanding stability. The boat performs best in brisk winds when she gives a fast and exciting performance. The pivoting rudder and lifting centreboard allow the boat to be launched in very shallow water and for towing, the beam, can be reduced to the width of a car. The boat is promoted by the RYA throught the 'Sailability' scheme.

DART 15

PN: 916 (PY)

LOA:	14'10"	4.54m
Beam:	6' 11"	2.13m
Draught:	0'10"	0.25m
Mast height:	variable	
Sail area:	110sq.ft.	10.19sq.m
Spinnaker:	none	
Weight:	231lb	105kg
Construction:	grp	
Designer:	Rodney Marsh	
Builder:	Laser Centre	
Rig:	una bermudan	
No. of crew:	two	

No. built / registered: 1,850

Class secretary: Tim Dieu de Belle-fontaine, The Malthouse, The Green, Steeple, Essex CMO 7RN

A versatile catamaran with exciting, yet easily managed performance sailed with a una rig or with the addition of a jib (22.6sq.ft./2.10sq.m.). This strict one-design class is the second largest catamaran class in the country, with fleets at over 20 locations. With the two-piece mast, the **Dart 15** is easily cartopped and quick and easy to rig: it is designed for a long life and is virtually maintenance free.

Using the same hull as the Dart 15, the **Dart Sting** has a slightly smaller mainsail area (109sq.ft./10.10sq.m.) with a unique reefing system and the provision of skegs instead of centreboards.

The **Dart 15 Sprint** (RN 880) has a fully-battened mainsail and furling jib.

DART 18 (INTERNATIONAL)

PN: 798 (PY)

LOA:	18'	5.48m
Beam:	7' 6"	2.28m
Draught:	0'10"	0.25m
Mast height:	26'3"	8.0m
Sail area:	173sq.ft.	16.08sq.m.
Spinnaker:	none	
Weight:	286lb	130kg
Construction:	grp	
Designer:	Rodney Marsh	
Builder:	Laser Centre	
Rig:	bermudan sloop with rotating mast	
No. of crew:	two	

No. built / registered: 7,235

Class secretary: Mrs Jane Stokes, Forest Gate Inn, Bell Common, Epping, Essex CM16 4DZ

Strict one-design high-performance double-handed catamaran class sailed with a rig on a rotating mast and a trapeze suitable for a wide range of crew weights, and ideal for couples. Singlehanded sailors can compete on equal terms with boats sailed two-up. The largest racing catamaran class in Britain there is a National and an International class association.

DART HAWK

PN: n/a

LOA:	18'	5.50m
Beam:	8' 6"	2.60m
Draught:	2'8"	1.0m
Mast height:	n/a	
Sail area:	220sq.ft.	20.45sq.m.
Gennaker:	205/235sq.ft.	
	19/21.8sq.m.	
Weight:	286lb	130kg
Construction:	grp	
Designer:	Yves Loday	
Builder:	Laser Centre	
Rig:	bermudan sloop	
No. of crew:	two	
No. built / registered: n/a		
Class secretary: n/a		

New high-performance catamaran with twin asymmetric hulls and an unique performance equalisation system which is easy to sail. The sophisticated rig control system is easily adjustable while the high volume hulls provide exceptional longitudinal stability.The **Hawk** is also available with a larger jib or gennaker.

DART 6000

PN: n/a

LOA:	19'6"	5.94m
Beam:	8' 3"	2.50m
Draught:	n/a	
Mast height:	n/a	
Sail area:	363sq.ft.	33.71sq.m.
Spinnaker:	none	
Weight:	398lb	180kg all up
Construction:	grp	
Designer:	Jo Richards	
Builder:	Laser Centre	
Rig:	bermudan sloop	
No. of crew:	two	

No. built / registered: n/a

Class secretary: n/a

High-performance catamaran designed in 1993 and sailed with a twin trapeze and an easily operated rig control system.

FORMULA 18

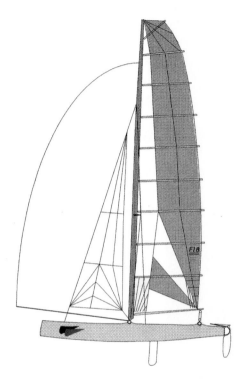

PN: n/a

LOA:	18'	5.52m
Beam:	8' 6"	2.60m
Draught:	4'	1.20m
Mast height:	29'6"	9.0m
Sail area:	220/228sq.ft.	
	20.45/21.15sq.m.	
Spinnaker:	204/226sq.ft.	
	19/21sq.m.	
Weight:	396lb	180kg
Construction:	grp	
Designer:	Dr Martin Fischer &	
	Roland Gabler	
Builder:	Race'nsail	
Rig:	bermudan sloop	
No. of crew:	two	
No. built / registered: new class		
Class secretary:c/o Race'nsail		

The first German contribution to the world's fastest growing catamaran class, the F 18 has been developed by the 1996 world tornado champion Rowland Gabler and catamaran specialist Martin Fischer.

HOBIE CAT 15

PN: n/a

LOA:	16'	4.90m
Beam:	7' 9"	2.38m
Draught:	10"/2'	0.27/0.63m
Mast height:	23'7"	7.20m
Sail area:	161.6sq.ft.	
	15sq.m.	
Spinnaker:	optional	
Weight:	363lb	165kg
Construction:	grp	
Designer:	Hobie Cat	
Builder:	Hobie Cat	
Rig:	bermudan	
No. of crew:	two to five	

No. built / registered: n/a

Class secretary: Tony Rix

24, The Brow, Friston, East Sussex

BN20 0ES

A family catamaran, with room for up to five, rigged with a boomless loose-footed reefable main on a rotating mast and sailed with twin trapezes. The symmetric buoyant hulls have a unique patented keel giving good pointing ability and minimal draught and kick-up rudders. The catamaran is cartoppable and easy to assemble and the mast is available in two pieces. An asymmetric spinnaker is available as an optional extra. The **Hobie 15** is very popular with teaching establishments.

HOBIE CAT 16 (INT.)

PN: 802 (PY)

LOA:	16'9"	5.11m
Beam:	8'	2.41m
Draught:	9"/1'11"	0.25/0.60m
Mast height:	26'	7.92m
Sail area:	218sq.ft.	20.26sq.m.
Spinnaker:	80sq.ft.	7.43sq.m.
Weight:	217lb	145kg
Construction:	grp	
Designer:	Hobie Alter	
Builder:	Hobie Cat	
Rig:	bermudan	
No. of crew:	one/two	

No. built / registered: over 100 000
worldwide

Class secretary: Tony Rix
24, The Brow, Friston, East Sussex
BN20 0ES

Most popular in the Hobie range, this is a strict one-design International class with asymmetrical hulls, raised platform for dryer sailing and an automatic and adjustable rudder system. Sailed with a double trapeze, an asymmetric spinnaker can be used to enhance downwind speed although it is not yet class legal.The **Hobie 16** is ideal for sailing schools and families and is raced worldwide. For beginners and sailing schools, the boat is available in the Easy and Junior versions with a smaller sail area of 113sq.ft./10.50sq.m. (Easy) or 81sq.ft./7.50sq.m. (Junior) and a jib of 40sq.ft./3.70sq.m.

HOBIE CAT 17 (INT.)

PN: 777 (SY)

LOA:	17'	5.18m
Beam:	8'	2.44m
	12'	3.66m with
	wings	
Draught:	6.5"	0.17m
Mast height:	n/a	
Sail area:	181sq.ft.	16.84sq.m.
Spinnaker:	none	
Weight:	330lb	156kg
Construction:	grp	
Designer:	Hobie Cat Europe	
Builder:	Hobie Cat Europe	
Rig:	bermudan	

No. of crew: one/two

No. built / registered: n/a

Class secretary: Tony Rix

24, The Brow, Friston, East Sussex

BN20 0ES

High-tech singlehanded sports catamaran which is simple to handle and easy to sail. Sailed with wings for dry and safe all round cruising or a trapeze for extreme conditions: an optional jib and boomless mainsail system can be added for sailing two-up or cruising. There is a comprehensive racing calendar.

HOBIE 20

PN: n/a

LOA:	19'4"	5.95m
Beam:	8'2"	2.50m
	9'6"'	2.90m with wings
Draught:	7"/2'6"	0.19/0.79m
Mast height:	29'6"	9m
Sail area:	231sq.ft.	21.4sq.m.
Spinnaker:	optional	
Weight:	418lb	198kg
Construction:	grp sandwich	
Designer:	Hobie Cat	
Builder:	Hobie Cat	
Rig:	bermudan	
No. of crew:	two	

No. built / registered: n/a

Class secretary: Tony Rix

24, The Brow, Friston, East Sussex
BN20 0ES

Strict one-designwith twin-trapeze, sports wings and asymmetric spin-naker. The square top tri-radial Mylar fully-battened main and jib give power and performance and there is a retractable centreboard system. There is a comprehensive racing circuit.

Hobie Tiger 18'/5.51m LOA designed for open formula 18 racing. The **Hobie Tiger** has a tri-radial Mylar mainsail of 183sq.ft./17sq.m., a jib of 37/45sq.ft./3.45/4.15sq.m. and a spinnaker of 205/226sq.ft./19/21sq.m. and is sailed with a crew of two/three and a double trapeze.

HOBIE WAVE

PN: n/a

LOA:	12'11"	3.96m
Beam:	6'11"	213m
Draught:	10"	0.28m
Mast height:	20'	6.10m
Sail area:	94.8sq.ft.	8.80sq.m.
Spinnaker:	none	
Weight:	74.8lb	34kg
Construction:	grp	
Designer:	Morell & Melvin	
Builder:	Hobie Cat USA	
Rig:	bermudan	
No. of crew:	two	

No. built / registered: new class

Class secretary: n/a

New fun catamaran ideal for families and beginners which is easy to rig and sail and cartoppable and which aims to open up cat sailing to a wider market. The **Wave** is rigged with a loose-footed high cut radial main with a jib as an optional extra. She is fast, responsive and safe to sail, with deep buoyant hulls with built in cushions and a flotation bulb at the top of the mast to prevent total inversion. Ashore, the kick-up rudders enable easy beaching and the hulls are low maintenance.

HURRICANE 5.9

PN: 691

LOA:	19'5"	5.9m
Beam:	8'	2.43m
Draught	n/a	
Mast height:	30'	9.17m
Sail area:	237sq.ft.	22sq.m.
Spinnaker:	none	
Weight:	271lb	123kg
Construction:	grp sandwich	
Designer:	Reg White	
Builder:	Topper Int.	
Rig:	bermudan	
No. of crew:	two	

No. built / registered: 500 +

Class secretary: Julia Machin,
207 Rosendale Road, West Dulwich,
London SE21 8LW

One-design twin-trapeze catamaran developed from the **Tornado** (see p.172) which aims to put high-performance cat sailing within the reach of all sailors. The pre-bent mast allows greater sail control of the powerful rig thus enabling crews with a combined weight of 18stone/114kg or above to handle the boat in most conditions and the kick-up rudders and centre-boards limit the risk of damage and enhance manoeuvrability.The **Hurricane 5.9** has a beam of only 8'/2.44m which allows it to be towed without dismantling: however the newly available **Sport** version is equipped with racks which should enhance performance in strong winds, and a spinnaker of 226sq.ft./21sq.m.

NACRA 6M

PN: 691 (RN)

LOA:	20'	6.0m
Beam:	8' 6"	2.59m
Draught:	5"/3'2"	12.5/96cm
	boards up/down	
Mast height:	31'7"	9.63m
Sail area:	255sq.ft.	23.65sq.m.
Spinnaker:	none	
Weight:	425lb	193kg
Construction:	grp	
Designer:	Performance	
	Catamarans Inc.	
Builder:	Performance	
	Catamarans Inc.	
Rig:	bermudan sloop	
No. of crew:	two	

No. built / registered: 375 +

Class secretary: Nick Greenwood

155, The Street, Monkton, Ramsgate, Kent.

Largest in a range of high-performance American-built catamarans sailed worldwide. The very high power-to-weight ratio makes these catamarans very fast yet they remain manageable due to the innovative control system. There is a fully-battened Mylar main.

SHEARWATER (NATIONAL)

PN: 839 (RN)

LOA:	16'6"	5.05m
Beam:	7' 6"	2.25m
Draught:	2'5"	0.75m
Mast height:	23'6"	7.20m
Sail area:	163sq.ft.	14.50sq.m.
Spinnaker:	190sq.ft.	17.64sq.m.
Weight:	265lb	120kg
Construction:	cold-moulded ply, grp, composite	
Designer:	Rowland & Francis Prout	
Builder:	Solite Sailboats (wood), Ian Ridge (grp)	
Rig:	bermudan sloop	
No. of crew:	two	

No. built / registered: 1,996

Class secretary: Ron Norman, 20, Palmerston Way, Alverstoke, Gosport, Hants PO12 2LZ

A development class which celebrates its 40th anniversary in 1997, the **Shearwater** has one-design hulls and a large sail area and is sailed with a double trapeze. It is fast and exhilarating to sail and performs well in rough weather. Variations in rig and deck layout are permitted.

TORNADO (INTERNATIONAL)

PN: 693 (RN)

LOA:	20'	6.10m
Beam:	10'	3.05m
Draught:	2'	0.61m
	(plate down)	
Mast height:	30'	9.10m
Sail area:	235sq.ft.	21.83sq.m.
Spinnaker:	195sq.ft.	18sq.m.
	(optional)	
Weight:	276/319lb127/145kg	
Construction:	grp/epoxy-nomex/ply	
Designer:	Rodney March (1967)	
Builder:	Reg White Ltd.	
Rig:	bermudan sloop	
No. of crew:	two	

No. built / registered: 400 in UK

Class secretary:Duncan Simmonds, 56 St Neots Rd, Eaton Ford, St Neots, Cambs PE19 3HN

Granted International status in 1976, this high-performance two-man catamaran has been the Olympic class catamaran since 1976. The **Tornado** is a fast racing catamaran with a very high-aspect ratio rig with a fully-battened sail, the battens projecting from the leach of the sail and is demanding to sail. The optimum overall crew weight is 21stone/135kg.There are active fleets worldwide with several in the UK.

UNICORN (NATIONAL)

PN: 775 (SY)

LOA:	18'	5.49m
Beam:	7' 6"	2.3m
Draught:	n/a	
Mast height:	26'	7.93m
Sail area:	140sq.ft.	13sq.m.
Spinnaker:	none	
Weight:	132lb	60kg
Construction:	ply/grp	
Designer:	John Mazotti	
Builder:	Unicat, Gary Piper	
Rig:	flexible	
No. of crew:	one	

No. built / registered: 1,094

Class secretary: Mrs Tanya Piper,
Windy Ridge, 89 Crofton Lane,
Hill Head, Fareham, Hants
PO14 3QE

Designed in 1967, the **Unicorn** is a high-performance singlehanded 'A' class catamaran sailed with a trapeze.The lightweight hull is one design and can be trailed assembled and the rig is flexible with a loose footed fully-battened sail. The boat can be home built from plans supplied by the RYA.

WARP

PN: n/a

LOA:	18'	5.48m
Beam:	7' 6"	2.30m
Draught:	1'	0.30m
Mast height:	26'3"	8.0m
Sail area:	196sq.ft.	18.20sq.m.
Spinnaker:	198sq.ft.	18.40sq.m.
Weight:	319lb	145kg
Construction:	grp	
Designer:	Dr Martin Fischer	
Builder:	Race'nsail	
Rig:	bermudan sloop	
No. of crew:	two	
No. built / registered: n/a		
Class secretary:n/a		

New 18' beach catamaran which is easily sailed singlehanded or two-up with a watertight wing profile mast, radial cut Mylar mainsail and double trapeze: an asymmetric spinnaker can be added. Similar in price and performance level to the **Dart 18** (see p.160) and **Hobie 16** (see p.165), the **Warp** has a distinctive canoe-style bow designed to give a drier sail.

FOURTEEN

Photograph by Warwick Baker - Shoreham by Sea

Aldeburgh Lapwing 12'6"/3.8m LOA 4'8"/1.4m BEAM
Designed by Morgan Giles in 1947 for the Aldeburgh YC the Lapwing one-design is a smaller version of the Thames Estuary OD. Open-decked and clinker built, she is bermudan rigged with a sail area of 100 sq.ft./93 sq.m. and there is a junior version with a reduced sail area of 75 sq.ft./6.96 sq.m. available. There is a fleet of 73 Lapwings still sailing.

Bembridge Redwing 27'11"/8.5m LOA 5'6"/1.7m BEAM
The original 1896 design by Charles Nicholson was replaced by a later one in 1938 and the class is one of the oldest one-design classes in the world. Although there are strict controls on the hull shape there is only one on the rig, namely that the total sail area should not exceed 200 sq.ft./18.6 sq.m.: a rule which in the past encouraged innovation in rig design and technology although now most Redwings are bermudan rigged. Her over-hanging stern and long shallow keel, suitable for navigating the shallow waters off Bembridge, and red sails make her a distinctive sight in the Eastern Solent. In 1990 there were still 28 boats sailing at Bembridge.

Broads One-Design 24'/7.3m LOA 5'1"/1.6m BEAM
Known locally as the 'Brown Boats' this one-design with gaff sloop rig of 262 sq.ft./24.3 sq.m. was designed by Linton Hope in 1900 for the Royal Norfolk & Suffolk YC. The mast is housed in a tabernacle to facilitate lowering and she is capable of being raced both on the Broads and on the open sea. Boats are now built in grp.

Conway One-Design 20'/6.1m LOA 6'7"/2m BEAM
Designed for the Conway YC by W. H. Rowland in 1928. This one-design class has a fixed keel and low aspect ratio bermudan rig, the boom projecting over the stern. Carvel built and three-quarter decked with a flat bilge, a sail area of 213 sq.ft./ 19.8 sq.m. is carried with a spinnaker set inside the forestay if required. Boats are now being built in grp.

Daring 33'/10.06m LOA
Keelboat designed by Arthur Robb approximately to the 5.5m rule, unique to Cowes, where it is sailed at The Royal Yacht Squadron. The class is a strict one-design, built in grp and is sailed with a large spinnaker which gives her excellent performance.

Dorado 12 12'6"/3.81m LOA 4'8"/1.4m BEAM (see page 175)
General purpose grp simulated clinker dinghy suitable for rowing, sailing or motoring with an easily managed lug or gunter sloop rig of 100sq.ft./ 9.3sq.m. Built by Dorado Boats, the Dorado Twelve is based on a 1912 design by George Cockshott and has room for up to four people

Duckling 9'8"/3m LOA 4'0"/1.2m BEAM
Small one-design wooden dinghy with a sail area of 54sq.ft./5sq.m. designed by Uffa Fox with characteristic rounded hull and built by Fairey Marine using the cold-moulded method. A gunter rig enabled the spars to be stored inside the boat for easy transportation. The Duckling was a very popular starter boat in the 1960s in which a generation of children learnt to sail.

Eleven + 11'0"/3.35m LOA 4'7"/1.4m BEAM
Small racing dinghy with double-chine hull originally designed for home construction in plywood although later hulls are grp. With a bermudan rig and sail area of 70 sq.ft./6.5 sq.m. the Eleven + is a fast safe and dry sea boat suitable for a crew of two.

Escape 11'6"/3.5m LOA 4'10"/1.48m BEAM
A revolutionary sailboat which enables beginners to sail solo very quickly. A smartrig system with just two control lines and a stepped-up boom takes only five minutes to rig. The una rig has a sail area of 81sq.ft./6.3sq.m.

Explorer 14'9"/4.5m LOA 5'8"/1.73m BEAM
Dinghy designed by Jack Holt and introduced by '*Yachting World*' in 1961 as a build-it-yourself grp dinghy suitable for cruising, racing or camping. The rig was gunter or bermudan with a sail area of 110 sq.ft./10.2 sq.m.

Falcon 16'6"/ 5.03m LOA 5'11"/1.80m BEAM
Uffa Fox designed wooden dinghy built by Fairey Marine in hot-moulded veneer. The **Falcon** is a well-decked family cruising boat with a steel centreboard designed for two to four people, with a bermudan sloop rig of 125sq.ft/11.60sq.m.

Falcon 16'0"/4.88m LOA 5'8"/1.73m BEAM
Open wooden clinker one-design of 1927 designed by W L. Bussell and sailed at Weymouth, with a bermudan rig and sail area of 150 sq.ft./14 sq.m. Out of the 50 built only 14 now remain

Fife One-Design 24'4"/7.42m LOA 6'4"/1.9m BEAM
One-design designed by William Fife in 1926 for the Royal Anglesey YC and built by Dickies of Bangor. Originally wooden, the class has a long keel, a long bow and counter stern with a bermudan rig and sail area of 250 sq.ft./23 sq.m. Boats are now being built in grp.

Hoylake Opera One-Design 16' /4.88m LOA 6'/1.8m BEAM
Designed by Alec Latta in 1902 with a flattish bottom and centreboard for sailing in the shallow Hoylake Channel these three-quarter decked boats

have a high peaked loose-footed lugsail and tiny jib set on a bowsprit with a sail area of 146 sq.ft./13sq.m.and a spinnaker of 62sq.ft./5.8sq.m. All boats in the class carry the names of operas.

International Lightning 19'/5.79m LOA 6'6"/1.98m BEAM
First launched in 1938, this one-design daysailer was designed by Sparkman and Stephens and rapidly gained worldwide popularity as a stable and simply constructed boat with a centreplate, that can be raced. Sail area is 177.5 sq.ft./16.5 sq.m with a spinnaker of 300sq.ft./28sq.m. to give excitement.

Jollyboat 18' /5.5m LOA 5'2"/1.57m BEAM
Uffa Fox design from 1953, developed from the early **International 14s**, which won the cross-channel dinghy race in 1956: originally built by Fairey Marine in moulded ply but now built in grp. The Jollyboat has a characteristic round bottom and is decked, with a tall mast and spreaders. Rigged as a bermudan sloop, she is sailed with a genoa, spinnaker and trapeze by a two-man crew. A heavy-weather boat she performs best in a good blow, when she is very fast.

Jollyboat 15' /4.6m LOA
Laurent Giles design - a daysailer with a grp hull available as a kit, part-built or ready to sail.

Kielder 12' /3.7m LOA 4'10"/1.47m BEAM
GRP simulated clinker dinghy gaff-rigged with a sail area of 96 sq.ft./ 8.9 sq.m. built by McNulty Boats and ideal for cruising. The smaller 9'0"/2.74m Kielder has a balanced lug rig and is ideal for children or to use as a tender. The gaff-rigged Kielder 16 18'3"/5.56m LOA is a family dayboat.

Loch Long One-Design 21'0"/6.4m LOA 5'10"/1.8m BEAM
Carvel-built one-design based on a Scandinavian design, with a small cuddy and a bermudan rig of 160sq.ft./15sq.m. The class is actively raced (PN: 1166 (RN)) with a large fleet at Aldeburgh as well as several in Scotland

Lymington River Scow 11'4"/3.45m LOA 4'11"/1.5m BEAM
GRP hull based on a traditional design from 1800s (see **Keyhaven Scow** p.87) which can be rowed, motored or sailed with a balanced lug rig with a sail area of 65 sq.ft./6 sq.m. and an optional jib. Built by John Claridge Boatbuilders.

Mayfly 12'9"/ 3.89m LOA 5'6"/1.68m BEAM
One-design, two-man hard-chine dinghy designed in 1956 by J. V. Kelley for marine ply construction but now built in grp or composite. A stable and seaworthy craft for racing and cruising, there is a sail area of 90 sq.ft./8.36 sq.m. with an optional spinnaker of the same area.

Menai Straits One-Design 20'/6.1m LOA 6'9"/2m BEAM
Designed in 1936 by W. H. Rowland, this flush-decked sloop is three-quarter decked with a centreplate and low aspect ratio bermudan rig and sail area of 212 sq.ft./19.7 sq.m. and is sailed by a crew of three.

Mermaid 11'0"/3.35m LOA 4'9"/1.45m BEAM
One-design wooden dinghy built by amateurs using the stitch and glue method and rigged as a gunter sloop with a sail area of 70 sq.ft./6.5sq.m.

Mersea Mylne One-Design 24'10"/7.5m LOA 7'0"/2.1m BEAM
Alfred Mylne designed these '18-Footers' in 1935 which are similar to the Fife One-Designs with a bermudan rig and a sail area of 250 sq.ft./23 sq.m.GRP hulls have been allowed since 1983.

Minisail 13'/3.9m LOA 3'8"/1.12m BEAM
Sailing surfboard with a scow-bow una rigged on an unstayed mast designed by Ian Proctor for beach launching. Safe, unsinkable and easy to sail with a sail area of 80 sq.ft./7.45 sq.m. it was very popular in the late 60s and 70s. Usually has a red or orange striped sail.

Norfolk Urchin 13'/4m LOA
New boat designed by Andrew Wolstenholme and built by the Norfolk Boatyard. A steady, safe boat with a gunter or cat rig and a sail area of 104 sq.ft./9.7 sq.m..

Pioneer 9'6"/2.90m LOA 4'6"/1.37m BEAM
A light-weight cartoppable polystyrene dinghy designed by Roland Prout: useful for family sailing with a sail area of 41 sq.ft./3.8 sq.m. sleeved on the mast or as a tender.

Puffin 7'6"/2.28m LOA 4'0"/1.21m BEAM
Collapsible-sided cartoppable dinghy designed by Barry Bucknell which weighs only 65lb/29.5kg. with a bermudan una rig. The 30sq.ft./2.78sq.m. sail sleeves on the tubular mast and the boat is suitable for sailing by children or for use as a tender.

Seabird Half Rater 20'/6.1m LOA 6'0"/1.8m BEAM
Oldest one-design class racing in Britain today: designed by Baggs and Hayward and built of pitch pine on oak with a centreplate, gunter rig and arched cockpit. Class established in 1898 and sailed at the West Lancs YC: 67 of fleet remain today.

Seaview Mermaid 24'6"/7.5m LOA 6'/1.8m BEAM
First British post-war one-design by Alfred Westmacott to replace an earlier design by G. V. Laws. The **Sunbeam** (see p.139) is an improved version of the Seaview Mermaid which is difficult to handle in heavy weather.

Skipper 14 14'/4.27m LOA 4'11"/1.5m BEAM
Cartoppable family dinghy for sailing and rowing with a deep and comfortable cockpit with a distinctive forward well. Designed in 1969 by Peter Milne, it weighs only 160lb/72.57kg and is rigged as a gunter sloop with a loose-bottomed sail sleeved on the gaff of 83.5 sq.ft./7.76 sq.m. There is also a **Skipper 12**.

Slipper 10'9"/3.45m LOA 4'7"/1.4m BEAM
Traditional pram sailing dinghy with a lightweight grp simulated clinker hull and mahogany thwarts, designed by Fred Gibbs in 1932. Bermudan rigged, she carries a sail area of 73sq.ft./26.5sq.m. and is built by Smith & Gibbs.

Star 22'7"/6.91m LOA 5'8"/1.73 BEAM
Two-man keelboat designed in 1918 with a hard-chine hull, and a bermudan rig with a sail area of 280sq.ft./26.5sq.m. Selected in 1932 as an Olympic class, the Star has remained so ever since apart from 1976 when she was briefly replaced by the **Tempest** (see p.144). GRP hulls were introduced in 1965.

Turtle 11'6"/3.5m LOA
GRP one-design with round bottom, foredeck and side benches, rotating mast and orange sails designed in 1970 by Thames Marine. Rigged as a bermudan sloop with a genoa and spinnaker she is sailed by a two-man crew.

Thames 'A' Class 27'/8.2m LOA 6'6"/1.98m BEAM
Class of wooden boats with a long overhang, heavy metal centreboard, tall bermudan rigged mast and large sail area of 320sq.ft./30sq.m. which is sailed at Thames SC at Surbiton. These boats are built to a formula whereby sail area multiplied by waterline length and divided by 6,000 must give a result between 0.8 and 1.0 so the boats are all slightly different.

West Kirby Star 16'9"/5.1m LOA 5'6"/1.7m BEAM
Class established by West Lancs YC in 1906 and designed by George Cockshott as an inexpensive boat suitable for youngsters and novices. These boats are half-decked and gunter rigged with an iron centreplate and distinctive red sails. The class was sold to the West Kirby SC in 1922 and by 1950 70 boats had been built.

Wight Scow 11'3"/3.4m LOA 4'9"/1.3m BEAM
One-design hull and sail with many variations on layout sailed on the South Coast and evolved for use in the solent tides. Originally built in wood, they are now built in grp (see **Keyhaven Scow** p.87, **Lymington River Scow** p.179).

Yare and Bure One-Design 20'/6m LOA 6'/1.8m BEAM
Class introduced in 1908 by the Yare and Bure SC. Smaller than the **Broads One-Design** (see p.177) these boats are known locally as the 'white boats' and are carvel-planked, gunter-rigged sloops with 275 sq.ft./25 sq.m. of sail. All are named after butterflies or moths.

Yorkshire One-Design 25'6"/7.8m LOA 6'9"/2.1m BEAM
Built in 1897 by Field & Co of Itchen Ferry to a design by J.S.Helyar these boats were originally gaff-rigged, changing to bermudan rig in 1973 and later adopting a Dragon-style cuddy. They are sailed at Bridlington.

BOATBUILDERS

Aldeburgh Boatyard
Fort Green
Aldeburgh
Suffolk
IP15 5DE

Tel: 01728 452019

Anglo Marine Services Essex Ltd
Wade Road
Gorse Lane Industrial Estate
Clacton-on-Sea
Essex CO15 4LT.

Tel: 01255 420717

Barker Brewer Boats Ltd
19 Coronation Road
Burnham-on-Crouch
Essex CM0 8HW

Tel: 01621 785316

The Barrow Boat Company
42 Barrington Place
Shepton Mallet
Somerset BA4 5GH

Tel: 01749 344038

Bassett Boatcraft
28 Bassett Gardens
North Weald
Essex
CM16 6DB

Tel: 01992 523262

Ron Beasley
2 Colliery Drive
Walsall
West Midlands WS3 2PL

Bell Woodworking Ltd
153 Parker Drive
Leicester LE4 0JP.

Tel: 0116 2340088

John Caig Sailcraft
71 High Street
West Molesey
Surrey KT8 2LY.

Tel: 0181 941 7473

Character Boats
Norwester Ltd
Unit 1
Rowlay Trading Estate
Allenby Road
Lytham St Annes
Lancashire FY8 2DG

Tel: 01253 727004

Chipstow Boatyards
Saxon Lodge, Oak Road
Downham
Billericay
Essex CM11 1QF.

Tel: 01268 710111

John Claridge Boatbuilders
Sadlers Farm Workshops
Lower Pennington Lane
Lymington
Hants SO41 8AL.

Tel: 01590 674821

C. M. Marine
105 Purewell
Christchurch
Dorset BN23 1EJ.

Comet Dinghies
Horsepond Meadow
South Molton
Devon EX36 4EJ.

Tel: 01769 574358

Concept International UK Ltd
Hill Farm
Radlett
Herts WD7 7HP

Tel: 01923 854681

Christopher J. Conway
32 Reymead Close
West Mersea
Essex
CO5 8DH

Cornish Crabbers Ltd
Rock
Wadebridge
Cornwall PL27 6PH.

Tel: 01208 86266

Brian Cory Boatbuilders Ltd
The Boatyard
Sandwich Industrial Estate
Ramsgate Road
Sandwich
Kent CT13 9LY.

Tel: 01304 613412

Coryn One-Design
24 Grosvenor Mews
Southampton Road
Lymington
Hants SO41 9JY

Tel: 01590 677448

Devon Yawl Ltd
Flagstaff House
Mudeford
Christchurch
Dorset BH23 3NP.

Don Marine Ltd
Lindon Road
Brownhills
Walsall
West Midlands WS8 7EB.

Tel: 01543 370018

Dorado Boats
Burnes Shipyard
Bosham
West Sussex PO18 8LJ.

Tel: 01243 576333

Estuary Sailboats
195 Park Road
Kingston upon Thames
KT2 5JY.

Giles Reinforced Plastics Ltd
1 Hatch Way
Kirtlington
Oxford OX5 3JS.

Tel: 01869 347801

Malcolm Goodwin
St Johns Road
Wivenhoe
Essex CO7 9DR.

Henshaw Inflatables Ltd
Bennetts Field Trading Estate
Wincanton
Somerset BA9 9DT.

Tel: 01963 33237

Heyland Marine
Bourne End Marina
Wharf Lane
Bourne End
Bucks SL8 5RR.

Tel: 01628 528830

Bob Hoare Racing Dinghies
35 Jumpers Avenue
Christchurch
Dorset BH23 2ER.

Tel: 01202 485708

Hobie Cat (Uk) Ltd
Potters Hall Business Park
Potters Green
Dane End
Ware
Herts SG12 0JU.

Tel: 01920 438555

Jack Holt Ltd
30 Lydden Road
Wandsworth
London SW18 4LR

Tel: 0181 870 9044

Honnor Marine (UK) Ltd
Drascombe Works
Dartington
Totnes
Devon TQ9 6DP.

Tel: 01803 862228

Itsa Marine
1 Denmark Road
West Cowes
Isle of Wight
PO31 7SY

Tel: 01983 293579

JEP Marine
Unit 17
Brents Boatyard
Upperbrent
Faversham
Kent ME13 7DL.

Tel: 01795 536032

Laser Centre
6 Riverside
Banbury
Oxon OX16 8TL.

Tel: 01295 268191

LDC Racing Sailboats Ltd
232 Hither Green Lane
London SE13 6RT.

Tel: 0181 852 3336

McNulty Boats
McNulty Quay
Corstophine Town
Commercial Road
South Shields
Tyne and Wear NE33 1RZ.

Tel: 0191 456 3196

Moores of Wroxham
Station Road
Wroxham
Norfolk NR12 8UT.

Tel: 01603 782294

Morton Boats
Eagle Road
Morton Swindery
Lincoln LN6 9HT.

Tel/Fax: 01522 868689

Nautivela
20139 Milano
Via Gardone 8
Italy

Tel: 02 55 21 21 16

Norfolk Boatyard Ltd
Tides Reach, The Street,
Morston
Nr Holt
Norfolk NR25 7AA.

Tel: 01263 740377

Northampton Sailboats
154-156 Balmoral Road
Kingsthorpe
Northampton NN2 6JZ.

Dave Ovington
Ovington Boats
Mariners Lane
Tynemouth
Tyne & Wear NE30 4AT

Tel: 0191 257 6011

Parker Racing Dinghies
61 Horseshoe Lane
Kirton
Boston
Lincs PE20 1LW.

Tel: 01205 723549

Performance Racing Sailboats
22b The Avenue
Flitwick
Beds MK45 1BP.

Petticrews
Burnham on Crouch
Essex

Porter Bros
Unit 1
Dewar Close
Segensworth West
Fareham
Hants PO15 5UB.

Tel: 01489 570222

Race'n Sail
Vertriebsgeses mbh
Kieler Strase 303
D-22525 Hamburg
Germany

Tel: 040/54 73 90 31

R.D.S. Ram Boats
61, Tetney Lane
Holton-le-Clay
Grimsby
DN36 5AS

Tel: 01472 220185

Red Fox Yachts Ltd
Pikes Hill Cottage
Pikes Hill Avenue
Lyndhurst
Hants SO43 7AX.

Tel: 01703 282616

John Reid and Sons Ltd
298-300 Reid Street
Christchurch
Dorset DH23 2BT.

Tel: 01202 483333

Ian Ridge
R.S. Fairings
Unit 6A Bury Farm
Curbridge
Southampton
Hants

RMW Marine
Rackfield Park
Broad Street
Ussculme, Cullompton
Devon EX15 3AX

Tel: 01884 841880

Rondar Boats Ltd
14 Indus Acre
Avro Way
Bower Hill
Melksham
Wilts SN12 6TP.

Tel: 01225 707550

Rowsell and Morrison
24 Camperdown Terrace
Exmouth
Devon EX8 1EH.

Tel: 01395 263911

7' Oaks Boats
81a Bradbourne Park Road
Sevenoaks
Kent TN13 3LQ

Severn Sailboats
3 Terne Road
Tolladene Road
Worcester
Worcs.WR4 9AE

Tel: 01905 22469

Brian Skinner
43 The Hills
Reedham
Norfolk NR13 3AR

Tel: 01493 700119

Smith & Gibbs
107 Latimer Road
Eastbourne
East Sussex BN22 7ET

Tel: 01323 723824

Tepco Boats
17-18 High Street
Leigh Old Town
Leigh On Sea
Essex SS9 2EN.

Tel: 01702 73770

Topper International Ltd
Kingsnorth Technology Park
Wotton Road
Ashford
Kent TN23 6LN

Tel: 01233 629186

Jon Turner
Turner Boats
Rull Bungalow
Ashill, Cullompton
Devon EX15 3LZ

Tel: 01884 840530

Victor Boats
112 Maldon Road
Burnham on Crouch
Essex CM0 8DB.

Tel: 01621 782603

West Solent Boatbuilders
The Boatyard
Keyhaven
Milford on Sea
Lymington
Hants SO41 0TE.

Tel: 01590 642080

Reg White
52 Seaview Avenue
Brightlingsea
Essex.

Guy Winder
Winder Boats
Canal Boatyard
Clyde Street
Bingley
West Yorks BD16 2NT.

Tel/Fax: 01274 568187

Woodnutt & Co Ltd
St Helens
Isle of Wight

Zephyr Sailboats
132 Sheffield Road
Dronfield
Sheffield S18 6GE.

Tel: 01704 542054

INDEX

Gull/ Gull Spirit	74	Lune Pilot 11'	101
Hawk 20	75	Lune Pilot 14'6"	102
Heron	76	Lune Whammel Boat	103
Heyland Lugger	77	Lymington River Scow	179
Heyland Swift	78	Marauder	104
Hobie 20	167	Mayfly	180
Hobie cat 15	164	Menai Straits One-Design	180
Hobie cat 16 (int.)	165	Merlin Rocket	105
Hobie Cat 17 (int.)	166	Mermaid	180
Hobie Tiger	167	Mersea Mylne One-Design	180
Hobie Wave	168	Mini-Moth	31
Hornet (National)	79	Minisail	180
Hoylake Opera One-Design	178	Miracle	106
Hurricane 5.9	169	Mirror (International)	107
International 10 sq metre canoe	81	Mirror 14	107
International 2.4 metre	80	Nacra 6m	170
International Lightning	179	National Eighteen	108
International Moth	82	National Twelve	109
Iso	83	Nimbus	110
Javelin	84	Norfolk One-Design	111
Jet	85	Norfolk Punt	112
Jollyboat	179	Norfolk Urchin	180
Kestrel	86	Ok (International)	113
Keyhaven Scow	87	Optimist	114
Kielder	179	Osprey (National)	115
Kinsman	155	Otter	116
Lark	88	Pacer	117
Laser (International)	89	Pegasus	118
Laser 13	93	Phantom	119
Laser 16	94	Pioneer	180
Laser 2 (regatta)	90	Puffin	180
Laser 4.7m	89	Raider 18	120
Laser 4000	91	Redwing (National)	121
Laser 5000	92	Royal Burnham One-Design	122
Laser Fun	90	Rs 200	123
Laser Pico	95	Rs 400	124
Laser Radial	89	Rs 600	125
Leader	96	Salcombe Yawl	126
Lightning 368	97	Scorpion	127
Loch Broom Post Boat	98	Seabird Half Rater	181
Loch Long One-Design	179	Seafly	128
Longstone 12	99	Seaview Mermaid	181
Lune Longboat	100	Sharpie	129